Halal If You Hear Me

The Breakbeat Poets Series

About the BreakBeat Poets series

The BreakBeat Poets series, curated by Kevin Coval and Nate Marshall, is committed to work that brings the aesthetic of hip-hop practice to the page. These books are a cipher for the fresh, with an eye always to the next. We strive to center and showcase some of the most exciting voices in literature, art, and culture.

BreakBeat Poets series titles include:

The BreakBeat Poets: New American Poetry in the Age of Hip-Hop, edited by Kevin Coval, Quraysh Ali Lansana, and Nate Marshall

This Is Modern Art: A Play, Idris Goodwin and Kevin Coval

The BreakBeat Poets Vol 2: Black Girl Magic, edited by Mahogany L. Browne, Jamila Woods, and Idrissa Simmonds

Human Highlight, Idris Goodwin and Kevin Coval

On My Way to Liberation, H. Melt

Black Queer Hoe, Britteney Black Rose Kapri

Citizen Illegal, José Olivarez

Graphite, Patricia Frazier

Commando, E'mon Lauren

BreakBeat Poets
Vol. 3

Halal If You Hear Me

Edited by Fatimah Asghar and Safia Elhillo

Haymarket Books
Chicago, Illinois

Published in 2019 by
Haymarket Books
P.O. Box 180165
Chicago, IL 60618
773-583-7884
www.haymarketbooks.org
info@haymarketbooks.org

ISBN: 978-1-60846-608-5

Distributed to the trade in the US through Consortium Book Sales and Distribution (www.cbsd.com) and internationally through Ingram Publisher Services International (www.ingramcontent.com).

This book was published with the generous support of Lannan Foundation and Wallace Action Fund.

Cover artwork, "Disco Baby," by Ayqa Khan.
Cover design by Brett Neiman.

Printed in the United States.

Library of Congress Cataloging-in-Publication data is available.

Table of Contents

II. SAWM

Safia Elhillo

Foreword: Good Muslim / Bad Muslim

I didn't have a Muslim community growing up because I was afraid. White people were mostly an abstraction for me as a child, and so was their judgement—a question about my accent here, a comment about my body hair there. They didn't know, early on, specific enough ways to really hurt me. The ones with that particular toolkit were my own people. A comment at Sudanese Sunday school about how I wore such tight jeans because I didn't have a father at home. Whispers about my divorced mother. My hair was this. My complexion was that. My Arabic, too this, too that. My family was this. I was too new, then too Americanized. I memorized their voices, anticipated their critique. This T-shirt was too short and revealed the roll of fat above my hips. This one was too tight and cupped my nonexistent breasts. I was a child, really—there was no reason for anyone to be looking at my body that way. But I would pull on a pair of jeans and anticipate eyes on the curve they made of my lower half. The way they molded to my ass. Or didn't. I spent most of my early adolescence swimming in fabric—a gray fleece Gap sweater that I wore every day, boys' cargo pants, oversize souvenir T-shirts my mother brought me from her travels. My own secular kind of covering. I didn't want anyone to look at me, to say anything.

As an adult, now with plenty of trauma at the hands of white people, the judgement I still fear the most is by those meant to be "my people." I screenshot horrible things Muslim men say to me on the Internet, and read and reread their messages into the night. I read and reread the comment left on a photo of mine, by a man I do not know, telling me in Arabic that my nose ring does not look good on me. The comment is so small, probably typed in passing. It takes over my entire day. I eventually delete it, but still cannot stop talking about it, months later. I have spent, really, my whole adult life and most of my adolescence, most of my childhood, trying to avoid being talked about in any capacity. "People will talk" was a governing principle in my upbringing, in my culture—a way of letting me know I should not do something (cut my hair short, wear clothes that are too tight, wear clothes that are too loose, be photographed with men, curse on the Internet, talk about my body, pierce my nose, double-pierce my ears, wear my hair in its natural curls to a wedding, wear a hoop nose ring), without giving the direct instruction.

I've been afraid, forever, of performing my identity incorrectly. My Muslimness, my Sudaneseness, my Americanness, my Blackness, my womanhood, all of it. I was a solitary kid, introverted and always reading, painfully shy. I looked to books to teach me how people *were* with each other—how they talked, how they touched, how they played, how they trusted, how they mourned. I practiced alone at night—jokes, pronunciations, nicknames I wanted people to give me. Tools of American girlhood like playing with my hair and keeping things in the back pocket of my jeans. I wasn't in any of the books I was reading—maybe a sliver here or there, a character with brown skin, with parents from somewhere else, with curly hair, but never the full extent of my intersection. I also wasn't seeing anyone ever talk about the nuances available in Muslim identity—at least not for women. I grew up watching men I knew drink and smoke and go to mosque, all in the same day. Their Muslimness felt like it made room for everything in their lives. The women I knew were not at all afforded this nuance—they were regarded either as religious or as secular. There was nothing in between. So I grew up hearing and using terms like "bad Muslim" and "good Muslim" and thinking of them as fixed identities. My first semester of college, I was scared and overstimulated and homesick and sad, and did not pray for months. And so I thought I was a bad Muslim, and thinking of myself as a bad Muslim allowed more months to pass without prayer, because praying started to feel like something I didn't deserve to do. I mourned my good Muslimness. I felt my whole life growing increasingly opaque outside to how Muslim I felt inside. I didn't have anyone to talk to about it. I'd meet new people who didn't know for months that I was Muslim. I'd meet other Muslims and obsess later about what they were saying about the fact that I'd been wearing shorts. I was very lonely.

The poems and essays in this anthology are the Muslim community I didn't know I was allowed to dream of. The Muslim community in which my child-self could have blossomed—proof of the fact that there are as many ways to be Muslim as there are Muslims. That my way was one of those ways, was a *way* of being Muslim that did count. The writers in this anthology demonstrate the sheer cacophony of Muslimness, of Muslim identities, of Muslim people. The range of things we're allowed to say and feel and want and mourn and joke about. We're accustomed, at this point, to media in which a cis, straight Muslim man gets to express his flawed Muslimness, to mess up and stray away and return and sin and repent and everything else that humans do. But the cisness, the straightness, the maleness of these voices has kept them safe in their expression of their flaws, in their trying to find their unique place within Islam. There are no stones for their bodies, no disownings, no honor killings. But what about a safe space for those who keep getting left out of the conversation about Muslims and Muslimness? How about populating the conversation in a way that's more representative of what the Muslim population actually looks like? My hope is that this anthology is a step in that direction. And that this anthology is a space where we don't have to be afraid of our own people, of being disqualified from our identities. Some freedom, albeit brief, from the governance of shame. This community has existed in our community all along, all over its margins.

Foreword: Finding the Hammam

The Salon was where I went to feel safe. Like the Planned Parenthoods across America, the Salon's exterior was unwelcoming, every inch of glass crowded in newspaper cutouts so you couldn't see inside. If you didn't know better, you'd think it closed.

It wasn't. Like Planned Parenthood, the newspapers across the glass were there to block out the outside world, to create a space where the women inside could not be seen by the men who owned the streets. Inside, behind two doors, The Salon was immaculate. The receptionist had beautiful curly black hair, and there were usually five or six women sitting around her, all sipping tea and discussing the latest in their lives. It was more of a mini-mall than a salon: there was a sugar-waxing studio, a nail salon, a gym, and a locker room with a Turkish bath (hammam) and showers, where the woman would gather, naked, in the water and talk for hours.

I had never been in a hammam before; I had joined The Salon simply because I wanted to use the gym and run on a treadmill freely in shorts without the risk of being harassed.

I was living in Jordan, studying abroad in Amman for a semester to better my Arabic. It was the first time my Pakistani-American ass was for real for real outside of the Western world, which despises Islam and Muslims. In my first few weeks in Jordan I'd been followed home twice from the bus by strange men hoping to marry me. My host brothers had to chase them out of our backyard. It became quite clear to me that I couldn't just walk outside freely without a man to help "protect" me. Places that were inside, with mostly women, became my only realm of real safety while I lived there.

It's not all that different from America. I was in middle school when the towers fell; my formative years were defined by the vitriolic racism and Islamophobia that plagued America in its wake. While most kids were worried about the sudden new stench of BO coming from their armpits, I was hiding in my school's bathrooms, afraid of being followed home or called a terrorist. I became used to harassment, not just in terms of race and religion, but also as a woman walking about the world. In my high school hallways I was regularly groped by the hands of young men when I was trying to get to class. Once, a classmate followed me out of class on my way to the bathroom and pinned me against a locker while he felt me up until I had to quite literally shout for him to get off me. He wasn't even reprimanded—the teacher who heard my scream just told us to stop goofing around and get back to class. The next day when I walked to the train station from school, he laughed with his friends and shouted, "You see those sideburns, dude? She has to be a fucking man, as hairy as she is."

Boys will be boys, as they say, and reap the benefits of a patriarchal world. A world that is built on "boys will be boys" violence; a world where women, femme, gender-nonconforming, trans, and queer people, by design, can never fit safely inside.

The street harassment in Jordan was only surprising to me because my naïve-self expected more from Muslim men. I was so excited to be living in a Muslim-majority place for the first time in my life, I hadn't even considered street harassment would happen. I expected it to more be like a family reunion, where we would all dance and sing together and practice Islam in whatever way that we saw fit. Aunties and uncles would greet me at the bus stop with sweets. We would all roll out our prayer mats in the streets and pray together, delighting in how our relationship with God was our own and free from judgment. That was far from the case. On sight, many people judged me as a haraami, a Muslim woman brimming with sin, going straight to hell. My uncovered (and often wet) hair, my sandals showcasing my exposed feet, and my western clothes were all sites of scorn.

This all changed in The Salon. In here, women took off their hijabs and the covered and un-covered blended in together without worry. Women talked openly about sex, showing each other lacy lingerie they had bought for a special night with their husbands. Bodies soaked in the warm water for hours as recipes were exchanged, and hair and nail tips were passed through the pools. I didn't feel judged; I just felt like I could come as I was, lose track of time, and spend hours just being. Here, for a few brief moments every day, we were free.

One day, the receptionist ran down the halls of The Salon flinging her hijab around her and screaming, "A man is here! A man is here! A man!" A maintenance man had come to fix a pipe that was broken in the building and was being sequestered between the two doors by non-hijabi women. The air shifted, the tension so thick it hung like a spoiled wedding cake throughout the complex. From corners I had never before noticed, women began pulling out shawls and draping themselves in them. A few women locked themselves in the waxing room, turning the light off and pressing themselves against the wall to avoid being seen, like the lockdown drills we practiced in middle school. Water splashed as wet bodies left the hammam, rolls jiggling with the force of running, emergency hijabs flying through the air. Within a minute, women who had previously been fully naked were completely covered, not a wisp of hair in sight.

I can't remember how long the maintenance man took. Ten minutes? An hour? We were all absolutely still, unmoving, not even the whirr of a treadmill going.

When he left, we all breathed freely again. And that is when I knew that this place was nothing short of magic. That I could live in The Salon, forever.

At a reading a few weeks ago, an audience member asked me how I would describe my poetics in a few words. I said I wanted them to be haraam-auntie poetics—the auntie who you can talk to about sex and sexuality, who you can go to when you can't go to your parents. Another audience member asked what I hoped my poems would do in the world. I told them that if one of my poems could make someone else feel seen, feel safe for a brief moment, feel a little less alone, I would have accomplished my goal. The two answers are really the same. Far too many times, I put myself in violent situations, particularly sexual, because I felt an aloneness, an otherness that I could not talk about with anyone. Because I could not name my desire. Because I could not reconcile the many things I was, within an identity that was accepted. Muslim. Pakistani. Kashmiri. American. Queer. Lower-class. Femme. Orphan. Sometimes woman. Sometimes man. Sometimes neither. Disposable.

What's the cost of a Muslim girl writing poems the way I do? I have already lost so much. What more can I stand to lose? It's the twenty-first century and we still live in a world of honor killings. A world where rape is rationalized. A world where trans women, particularly Black and brown trans women, are being murdered without justice. A world where police murder Black civilians and go unpunished. A world where the murders of Muslim people are not considered hate crimes. A world where queer people are thrown out of their homes. A world where girls are married off, before they can even name their own desire.

What's the cost, of writing poems the ways we do?

Join me. Join us. Let us create a poetics that recreates the hamaam, where we can come in our real, naked skin, sit in the water, and talk openly. Where all of us—the hijabis, the haraamis, the uncovered, the gender-nonconforming, the queer, the married, the never-married, the virgins, the non-virgins, the brown, the black, the white, the yellow—can just be. Can just be seen. Can just be heard. Can be celebrated. Can live, exist, and make our own freedoms.

I.
SHAHADA

Following the Horn's Call

Someone labeled a postcard of *The Last Supper*
"People Eating Food."

I laughed because a fish was only fish, bread only bread
until someone explained about Jesus.
In heaven there must be dinners.

If I could get close enough to any honorable table I would say,
Moses, I had trouble with *r*'s and *s*'s. How about you?
Did God unloose your tongue all at once?

Do they love Jonah or do they laugh at him?
Do they ask how many arches in the beast's mouth?
Did he count them like ceiling tiles?
Do they say, I trembled when the sea split.
When the flame spoke. When the one who plays the first note
of the last moment showed me his wings?

Do all the women cut their palms because of Joseph's beauty?
Does he ever smile at his own face in the cutlery?
I want to see him and compare him to the others.

Paradise is to ask whatever you like. A tea with God.
I have filled a book with questions I can't remember.

I'm Trying to Stop Writing About Water

But a girl lets her lip hang
the whole morning prayer.
"We let our dresses drag,"
my cousin has said for years.
"We are devout."
A woman, then her mother,
wipes the girl's drool.
It falls into her palm,
onto her white patent shoes.
Between the rows,
boys in cream and gold, unsure
if they want to be on the men's side,
or with their mother,
whose embroidery matches theirs.
When they turn, there are fold lines
down their backs and legs.
I leave lines on my own back,
wonder at my unborn labor.
The girl drools onto pink stockings.
However her mother adjusts them,
they turn on her heels.
They smile at her heels.
When the children become restless,
a woman claps, sharp,
and they all look at her, accept a lull,
then laugh and crawl between rows,
across rows. The children make
their own row. They crowd
around the white patent shoe.
The mother turns the shoe over
and smiles at its sole.
She wears it on her fingers,
loans it to her girl. The girl takes it
with both hands, strokes its strap.
When restless, again,
her mother lifts her black robe,

4 walks her fingers over and over
a green skirt, the color of grass
in a soaked field,
grass between pools,
in roadside forests. Abrupt.
Contained. They gather fabric
in their fingers, then their fists,
pulling both robe and skirt up, up.

Aisha Sharif

Why I Can Dance Down A Soul-Train Line in Public and Still Be Muslim

My Islam be black.
Not that "Don't-like-white-folks"
kind of black. I mean my Islam be
who I am—black, born and raised
Muslim in Memphis, Tennessee,
by parents who converted
black. It be my 2 brothers
and 2 sisters Muslim too
black, praying at Masjid Al-Muminun,
formally Temple #55,
located at 4412 South Third Street
in between the Strip Club
and the Save-A-Lot black.
My Islam be bean pie black,
sisters cooking fish dinners
after Friday prayer black,
brothers selling them newspapers
on the front steps black, everybody
struggling to pay the mortgage back
black.

My Islam be Sister Clara Muhammad School
black, starting each day
with the pledge of allegiance
then prayer & black history
black. It be blue jumpers
over blue pants, girls pulling bangs out
of their hijabs to look cute
black. My Islam be black & Somali
boys and girls, grades 2 through 8,
learning Arabic in the same classroom
cuz we only had one classroom

black. It be everybody wearing a coat inside
cuz the building ain't got no heat
black.

My Islam be the only Muslim girl
at a public high school
where everybody COGIC asking sidewise,
What church you go to?
black. It be me trying to explain hijab
black, *No, I don't have cancer. No,*
I'm not a nun. No, I don't take showers
with my scarf on. No, I'm not
going to hell cuz I haven't accepted
Jesus Christ as my Lord and Savior
black. My Islam be riding on the city bus
next to crackheads and dope boys
black, be them whispering black,
be me praying they don't follow me home
black.

My Islam don't hate Christians
cuz all my aunts, cousins,
and grandparents be Christian
black. It be joining them for Easter
brunch cuz family still family
black. My Islam be Mus-Diva
black, head wrapped up,
feathered and jeweled black. It be me
two-stepping in hijab and four-inch heels
cuz dancing be in my bones
black.

My Islam be just as good as any Arab's.
It be me saying, *No, I ain't gonna pray*
in a separate room cuz I'm a woman
black. And, *Don't think I can't recite Qur'an too.*
Now pray on that black!

My Islam be universal
cuz black be universal.
It be Morocco and Senegal,

India and Egypt. My Islam
don't need to be *Salafi*
or *Sufi*. It don't have to be
blacker than yours black.
My Islam just has to be.

An Introduction

my god wakes up with bed head
and sticky fingers, doesn't
want to go in to work today

my god forgets to do the dishes
lets all the houseplants die

my god teenages
built this earth on Friday night
and tires of it on Sunday morning

my god commands
a willing army, unwillingly
mutters, whines

my god is so type B
just wants to be left alone
just wants to smoke a cigarette
and not think of the parents and their children

my god is a liar
always one foot out the door
and ready to leave me here
if that's what it takes

my god fickles
breaks every bony promise
picks away at the meat
laughs when i tantrum

still, i half-kneel and pray a half-prayer
bend until i can look myself in the eye
still, there is no god but God
so i make do with this one

Rumsha Sajid

Muslim Girl Preamble

We the sisters of every color
in order to form a more perfect union
establish the sanctity
of elbows touching between women
while standing in prayer.
We preserve justice
through tucking our
homegirl's stray hair
back into her hijab when
she doesn't notice her ponytail is out.
During Ramadan
when our periods sync up
we will go
out for lunch together.
By the powers vested in us
we will not be called
last to eat at the fam jam
or let you expect us
to babysit aunties' kids at the mosque.
We secure our sisterhood
by knowing there is enough
baraqah for us all
therein never comparing our noor
with another sister's.
We solemnly swear to never silence
ourselves for your comfort
and support each other's journey
to peace from
this dunya to
the akhira.
Insha'Allah.

Glory Be to the Gang Gang Gang

In praise of all that is honest, call upon the acrylic tips
and make a minaret out of a middle finger, gold-dipped
and counting. In the Name of Filet-O-Fish, pink lemonade,
the sweat on an upper lip, the backing swell and ache,
of Abdul Basit Abdus Samad on cassette tape, a clean jump shot,
the fluff of Ashanti's sideburns, the rice left in the pot,
the calling cards and long waits, the seasonal burst
of baqalah-bought dates.

Every time they leave and come back
alive.

Birthmarks shaped like border disputes.
Black sand. Shah Rukh's dimples, like bullets,
taking our aunts back to those summer nights,
these blessings on blessings on blessings.

Give me the rub of calves,
rappers sampling jazz,
the char of frankincense,
and everything else that makes sense
in a world that don't.

Jesus at Wynfield Station

Remember 1997 when we were here
a year in this new country, every limb
an instrument we could not make sing?

Our small girl bodies felled and risen
from the dead until we found our feet
and ran?

We did not know how to walk in this new skin
blackening suddenly before us until our brothers
brave and braggadocios,

taught us how to Nigger with our mouths leaning,
our tongues sneak full
of all the clanging they claimed to be English.

What mama called *no language at all.*
No culture, neither.

Remember mama, and the roaches?
How they overran the house, flew over our heads?

And all seven of us, huddled in the empty of our living room waiting
while she swatted with bare hands at

everything—the ceiling, our feet, her own nervous trembling mouth

until, finally, the white man arrived and she led him
to the bathroom where we watched as he jumped back
pink with fright.

JESUS!

and they came forth: a sea of small black roaches
crawling towards the light.

Yes! Jesus! mama said,
Jesus fly-fly everywhere!

And everywhere Jesus flew we found ourselves
what we must have looked like at the border
naked and black and trembling, the years
splayed open-legged before us.

Each one a small war we entered hoping this time
to survive.

Paulander Drive

for girls with glossy lips and big hoop earrings
slick kicks
low riders
&
kissed teeth

for kids who run but never walk
soles of feet
thick rubber
&
hot pavement beneath

for sisters sat
shoulders to knees
hair parted
&
coconut oil and corn rows

for mamas huddled in kitchens
folded sambusas
belly laughs
&
hot tea

for brothers, posted up in threes
jerseys
du-rags
&
white tees

for streets that stay lit long after sunset
&
worlds inside one another

Small Talk

you michelangelo's crouching boy/ you d'angelo's purr/ you dead currency/ you dead presidents/ you a stick of incense/ you a stick-up artist/ you haraami/ you the hum of a lifetime basined in my lap/ count our tallies of loss backwards for me/ run to the bank & translate it into a fistful of green of your choice/ or something else sanctified/ or european/ pick the synonym of your choice.

in a traditional sense/ the body holds its arithmetic/ exports it outwards/ to the touch and exhale/ the praxis felt best/ against a groan of concrete/ with the dumb weight of a hand against the small of a back/ here, an elevator is our only spiritual ascension/ can i be excused from living so slimly?

i dream you closer too/ besides the honey-coloured dog licking its vulva/ an abstract laugh swelling inside your throat/ ask me about blood clots and spun coins/ the cracked skin of heels/ anything but the nightly heartbreaks of/ too many addresses/ and all the ways/ i am still auditioning/ for this country's approval.

Asmarani Is at a Party & Knows This Song

i learn all the words to cam'ron's hey ma
i learn all the words to foolish   i learn
the words to big pimpin   & candy shop
this is how i became an american

i stockpile the words by a radio
in the cool lacuna of night   & each
new sound   blues my passport to mirror the
ocean's dark   rounds the song in my mouth

to a twang   & now i cannot remember
my wealth of middle names   the list of men
who had to live   for my father to
become my father   our house is silent

back home & its daughter is split clean down
the middle & must someday choose a side

Muslim Girlhood

I never found myself in any pink aisle. There was no box for me
with glossy cellophane like heat and a neat packet of instructions
in six languages. Evenings, I watched TV like a religion
I moderately believed. I watched to see how the others lived, not knowing
I was the Other, no laugh track in my living room, no tidy and punctual
resolution waiting. I took tests in which Jane and William had
so many apples, but never a friend named Khadija. I fasted
through birthday parties and Christmas parties and ate leftover *tajine*
at plastic lunch tables, picked at pepperoni from slices like blemishes
and tried not to complain. I prayed at the wrong times in the wrong
tongue. I hungered for Jell-O and Starbursts and margarine, could read
mono- and *diglycerides* by five and knew what *gelatin* meant, where it came from.
When I asked for anything good, like Cedar Point or slumber parties,
I offered a quick *Inshallah,* as in *Can Jordan sleep over this weekend, Inshallah?*,
peeking at my father as if he were a god. Sometimes, I thought
my father was a god—I loved him that much. And the news thought
this was an impossible thing—a Muslim girl who loved her father—
assumed every Muslim girl-heart was a bomb, her love
suspicious. But what did they know of my heart, or my father
who knew it, and so drove fifty miles to buy me a doll like a Barbie
because it looked like me, short brown hair underneath her hijab, unthreatening
breasts and feet flat enough to carry her as far as she wanted
to go? In my games, she traveled and didn't marry, devoured any book
she could curl her small, rigid fingers around. I called her *Amira*
because it was a name like my sister's, though I think her name
was supposed to be *Sara,* that drawled *A* so like *sorry,*
which she never, ever was.

Haram

God supports my waxing habit.
—Khudejha Asghar

The day Auntie A saw my sister's pussy
hairs crawling out & around her underwear
so long that if you ripped through the tangles
you could part them into pigtails
was the day we were all given our own
pair of scissors & told to read namaaz.
Your hairiness is against Allah's will
my Auntie scolded, the disappointment
lined on her too-young face. The three
of us sisters lined up to wash our feet
in the tub, our shame quieting us as the wadu
water splashed all the way to our arms.
Khudejha had to do Astaghfirullah, repenting
for her evils as we cut each lock
of hair, discarding them in a plastic bag
we got from the corner store
because they were too thick to flush down
our struggling toilet. The next day, we sisters
woke at 5am to read the Qur'an,
massacring the scripture in our American
mouths. We read the Surah about not painting
your nails or altering any part of your body
& wondered about our sheared bushes,
once a part of us & now finding shelter
in some smelly garbage. Maybe we misunderstood
the Surah. Maybe we were outside Allah's creations.
But we knew better than to question my Auntie's
law, almost its own Sharia in our apartment.
We speculated the Qur'an hadn't ever imagined
hairiness like ours, so vast, it was its own sin.

Self-Portrait as Mango

She says, "Your English is great! How long have you been in our country?" and
I say, "Suck on a mango, bitch, since that's all you think I eat anyway." Mangoes

are what model minorities like me know nothing about, right? Doesn't
a mango just win spelling bees and kiss white boys? Isn't a mango

a placeholder in a poem folded with burkas? But this one, the one
I'm going to shove down her throat, is a mango

that remembers jungles jagged with insects, the river's darker thirst.
This mango was cut down by a scythe that beheaded soldiers, mango

that taunts and suns itself into a hard-palmed fist only a few months
per year, fattens while blood stains green ponds. Why use a mango

to beat her to death? Why not a coconut? Because this "exotic" fruit
won't be cracked open to reveal whiteness to you. This mango

isn't alien just because of a bone-hard brown shell. I know
I'm worth waiting for and I want to be kneaded for ripeness. Mango:

my own sunset-skinned heart waiting to be held and peeled, mango I taught
myself to suck open with teeth. Tappai! This is the only way to eat a mango.

Say Love Say God

I liked the idea of an impossible love.
I was told a love so different can't
make children with souls
worth praying for. But those stories
in the Bible and the Qur'an,
love, we knew what they meant.
When you said *sin*, love, you did not
mean my legs, or the way
you were already inside me.
When you said *sin*, you meant
how one forgets. Do you remember
how we slept naked? You were there.

I believe love is immortal, irrational,
and sometimes, tired. The sun, it seems, worships only
the bodies of the young. When I say *old*,
I mean how far we've traveled, love, how we go
back. When I walk new cities, I always
think of you, love. I tell you, *Look—*
lives upon lives upon lives.
Sometimes heaven is when I'm away from you, love.
Sometimes heaven is only the two of us. I know you
understand. Only petty loves want to be worshipped.

I liked the idea of an impossible god.
I was told a god so different can't
make children with souls
worth praying for. But those stories
in the Bible and the Qur'an,
god, we knew what they meant.
When you said *sin*, god, you did not
mean my legs, or the way
you were already inside me.
When you said *sin*, you meant
how one forgets. Do you remember
how we slept naked? You were there.

I believe god is immortal, irrational,
and sometimes, tired. The sun, it seems, worships only
the bodies of the young. When I say *old*,
I mean how far we've traveled, god, how we go
back. When I walk new cities, I always
think of you, god. I tell you, *Look—*
lives upon lives upon lives.
Sometimes heaven is when I'm away from you, god.
Sometimes heaven is only the two of us. I know you
understand. Only petty gods want to be worshipped.

Nadra Mabrouk

Memory in Which We Are Not Singing but You Are Home

Early morning, my brother and I climb
to the roof of the building,
clouds of different languages
in the back of our dew-wet throats.
Here where our grandmother lived,
stuffed the glass I tried to chew
between sofa cushions,
we want to see how the streets
become fogged tunnels from above,
how the blurring heads of passersby
become different fabrics of colors
we have yet to name, tones bleeding
between synthetic, flammable strands.
The air is halved again, a revolution splintering
its feathery bones between us.
I can't fully hear the music from the street,
try to tilt my head, wait for it to get louder,
or just for you to reach across
before jumping.

Brother as Younger Self

The streets of Shobra are still traced
with music from years ago—
children ripping
the clothes off lines,
pins scattering in a rounded clatter
of sharp-throated wooden notes.
It might have been a merging
of Mohamed Fouad
or Mohamed Mohy
or Mohamed Fawzi,
and my brother (also a Mohamed),
is sitting in the shimmering corner
of our grandma's balcony with one leg up.
He wants to finish this one song
because it has his favorite parts
which he has rewound a few times now
& Mahmoud is downstairs again
yelling & holding a peeling board game
they taped together & my brother's eyes glint
over to the chorus, remembering how Mahmoud
once told him how his father comes home
only once a month, and he feels bad
he is taking so long to go downstairs
but this would be the last time
he rewinds the song, Mahmoud, *wallahi*,
he yells, the cassette player's volume
on high but not loud enough
to fully drown out the street market prices,
the chatter of bent men
at the coffeehouse, their fingers caterpillar-like
through the mug holders blowing
on clouded tea,
but the music is just enough
to shroud it all in the blur
of a filmy fog that Mahmoud can hear
and he can't help but to remember

how sometimes at night,
if he closes his eyes hard enough,
he hears the din of keys
against the door,
the whistling of a man
nearly always caught in
the middle of an
unfinished song.

When You're Brown with a Hand-Me-Down Bike

i don't know what her actual name was. i only remember her being the age of a woman much older than my brothers and i, her fist clenched in a way that drew my eyes to the girth of her palms leaking out of the inward curl of her fingers. shit, all that dirt under the nails. she had her other hand on the bike derek had given me when it was rusted enough for him to buy a new one. he was excited to turn it over to me and oh, was i ever excited to lean my whole torso into the handles and catch the wind with my mouth and eyes and the under of my arms. my brother held a basketball under his arms and shook and flinched while she told us we smelled and we should go back home. when the rust finally hit her feet and we had to submit to the walk back to the house in the sun's new spring, we did not say a word. my brother dribbled the ball, matted and worn against the concrete, and we heard her laugh with her boyfriend about what we didn't deserve. and i knew then we were dirty and i told hassam that a loss is only a loss if you really had to lose something. the bike was a free thing and without it, they couldn't take anything else. we were free things now, too. we were free and overflowing and i remember too much of that day. there was the dirt of our skin and the sweat on our foreheads and the relief of having nothing again. when i grabbed his arm and asked him to slow down and he saw that i had been crying, i remember he did all the work of the older brother. he talked of god and of morals and all that we were even when the world took things away from us. because what was the older girl but the world, a white hand taking and taking and taking and laughing as our backs receded into concrete horizon. he talked to me of forgiveness and somehow i forgot in my oldest age what it actually means. and it is a fickle thing. because derek came over one day later and told me he saw the bike leaning against a rusted white house a few blocks away, so i rallied and rallied and waited for my brother to jump on the wagon of vengeance. i recall only the thrill in him being extinguished by the obligation to again teach me the older brother's lesson. and again, he taught me forgiveness. and when he learns i am a man who loves men and glory and drink, he is more flawed than before. but still, he teaches me. i'll never forgive myself for forgetting the weight of another being lifted off my back. i'll never forget what it means to forgive.

& My Fathers Relived My Birth

Twelve years old and I was as bad as my aunts said. In Taza, we went to my uncle's wedding. We slept in a small hotel and I poured warm milk off the balcony. I stole all the chocolates from the front desk. I was kind to the bride but I cursed in English. I spit zuriya'ah seeds everywhere. I ate more than my share. *Aa'weeli, hashooma, Yasmin, baraka aleek.* This part is blurry: thick slaps of blood on the staircase. They slaughtered the cow on the roof before the wedding. Later that night, my uncles danced. In dreams, the cow comes back to life over and over, her eyes as dark as my own.

II.
SAWM

Fasting in Tunis

Longing, we say, because desire is full
of endless distances.

—Robert Hass

My God taught me hunger
is a gift, it sweetens
the meal. All day, I have gone without
because I know at the end I will
eat and be satisfied. In this way,
my desire is bearable.

I endure this day
as I have endured years of days
without the whole of your affection.
Your desire is one capable of rest.
Mine keeps its eyes open, stalks
through heat that quivers,
waits to be fed.

The sun burns a hole through
the sky and I am patient.
The ocean eats and eats
at the sand and still hungers.
I watch its wide blue tongue, knowing
you are on the other side.

What is greater: the distance between
these bodies, or their need?

Noon gapes, a vacant maw—
there is long to go
until the moon is served, white as a plate.
You are far and still sleeping;
the morning has not yet slunk into your bed,
its dreams so vast and solitary.

Once, long ago,
I touched you,
and I will touch you again—
your mouth a song
I remember, your mouth
a sugar I drink.

A Conversation with Ammi

On a Wednesday afternoon, over a cup of tea

my voice on the phone: *how do you cook eggplant*
with green chillies and onion seeds? In a city

three hours ahead, I empty out the fridge.
Dinner guests arrive at seven. Hold on, a UPS delivery

at the door. November feels abnormally warm—
swollen sunlight rubs down the windows.

In your version, I wear my hair long
married to a man with soft brown hands.

I never fall in love with a woman.

Nail Technician as Palm Reader

The nail technician pushes my cuticles
back, turns my hand over,
stretches the skin on my palm
and says *I see your daughters*
and their daughters.

That night, in a dream, the first girl emerges
from a slit in my stomach. The scar heals
into a smile. The man I love pulls the stitches out
with his fingernails. We leave black sutures
curling on the side of the bath.

I wake as the second girl crawls
head first up my throat—
a flower, blossoming
out of the hole in my face.

Creation Myth

Nothing here glitters,
hence it must be real. Like the plant I'm excising,
I am gouging & gorging on foreign limbs. So disgusted I am
with me; even the one-eyed hobo mourns,
his screech a wet scroll excavating the night.
Tonight I have to animal my hunger. God descends with her talons,
injects fat into my arm. Don't be afraid, come in.
Through the bleak of her iris, I enter: Am I beautiful
now? Does my scalp smell of shampoo? I am hell-wire
pulled and strung—my vertebrae all copper-din, blue as the sinner
who kilned them. God thumbs the cervix of me,
my peanut-wing unflapping—with you here, I am a limp goose, corn-oil
and drunk, a haft for abdomen. It is entirely laborious
to be woman, with my crotch of feathers, tongued
by this toga-ed slut of a moon. Tonight, I will never be holy or concave
enough. Is this party over soon? I cannot resume a sense of gratitude
—not with this body I'm crawling in. Consider the gremlins
under their umbrellas, all plastic syringes and thumbs
sprouting dollar-bills ad infinitum. I believed it all,
prayed to calories and crystal balls. Rolled up cigarettes, curled up inside
the carton of God's ear, salted
and fried year after year I spent in asceticism. Apologetic I am only for that brutish
sugar-cube, and your dick with its helix of lies, plummeting
on the wet-glazed couch crouched waterside—how those ponies
galloped through my arteries, each of their hoofs
fuming its own story,
echoing girl after girl crashing into a putrid canal.

Come Here Where Are You Going Come Here

When it all turns to dust that's when you know the stars begin.

I watched the rims of cups of tea rise to his lips *chfff.* They were oddly colored like purple *chff.* Bodies have names you know. That's the way it's always been. You may now wipe the spit off Noor's hair—if there's any of this you could do without doing: spit, wipe, hate a woman for having a body.

I never saw the oranges turn beyond green. We yanked them off dusty branches to stuff into our lips like limes. Got the skin beneath my nails and that's how I explained the blackness. Not dirt. Bodies don't always know why they're doing what they're doing you know. You may now unvomit the blood you tried to stop from spreading too far below the knees.

I felt as many mosquitoes on my sandaled feet as I saw rings of light carpeting the black above. It was a time before YouTube, you know. And we didn't know much about politics. (Well at least we didn't know it was *called* politics. And we didn't know it was a before—it was just a time.) That's why we squeezed toy girls with toy hair. I liked to sit beside the hibiscus and taste the watery sugar of its neck. Bodies don't always know what's coming, you know. You may now remove Barbie's head from your crotch but slowly, not like you've had enough. Had enough of what?

I never understood why there was hair even on my back. I pictured it growing so thick I could vanish nights without stars. They cooked halawa on the stove: sugar, water, lime and a spoon. Noor told me that young couples took turns. To make each other visible. To see not themselves, but each other. (She didn't say all that but this here's poetry.) You may now undream your big night—the dust's so dense you might be blind. Wait are your eyes closed? My eyes? Are they?

When you love a body you know what betrayal is. It is pretending our bodies are abstractions—so we could become dust and say our bodies were only ever stars.

Mama Says

Our wild, beautiful thickets and dense forests are God's greatest gifts. The long dark tendrils weave and cross over each other and blow in the wind. My Mama has always taught me to love it and care for it because it's my responsibility. She says "This is your blessing; these cornrows and bushes are yours. Don't ever take them for granted. It's your job to keep what you have healthy and to make sure it can grow; never forget that. God looked down on our people and blessed us with this, no one else has what we have so be grateful. And remember that your care will help it grow and your neglect will make it die, don't ignore it." I've learned that it's my job to maintain the beauty in my life. And as my Mama works with it making it more beautiful than it already was, I sit wondering what gorgeous thing she's done with my kinky, curly, frizzy, unique black girl hair.

Ammi

I love the sound
of cutting fabric.
Right sides embrace,
unfold into mirrored halves.
Gemini twinned brown mothers.
Coarse hairs plucked
from frayed double seams.

We don't sleep.
Bodies tense with listening
for whines coughs cries
or too much quiet.
We hide in bed with covers over our heads
sheets drawn tightly over our growing resemblance,
and pinned under our chins.
Mine is ripping at the juncture
as we stand
Prostrate
sit on our heels.

You gnawing on whispered verses,
slapping fat syllables with your tongue,
swallowing surahs for the angels who claw at your shoulders.
And before I can nudge *Assalamu alaikum wa rahmatullah*
through clenched teeth

you deliver me

out of your mouth with a gust of cool breath,
swaddle me in the hands of Fatima,
stain me with goat's blood.

Blooms Omen

The furrow in my brow
My mother once painted over
With the blood
Of a newly slaughtered sheep
For a blessing of good health
I never honored
Not because I want to be sick
But I'm the type to like
The smell of my blood
Better

The omen of blooming health
I trade for a sniff
Heady and solemn when
I rock back with it like a
Filled glass
Intoxicant
With my own poultice
A logic heating
A little space around me
Like an oven raising
Its warm-herbed, broken-shelled, nutty
Smear of smell.

Safia Elhillo

Ode to Swearing

now i know the worst profanity
what men use when they need to curse
one other to cut word i only know
as a swear *your mother's [ ]*

your sister's mine in arabic the word
hisses traps the tongue between the teeth
spits word so similar to an english
kiss turned to venom by inflection

to rot in the mouth site of shame
birthplace of the profane but what
word can i use to call my own how
without disgrace can i name my innocent parts

my wounds i am saying if asked
in arabic i could not tell you where i open

Hypothesis: Bitch Face

i don't think it's that black femmes glare when we're walking down the street.

but maybe this world's so close to hell that our heaven's gotta be inside our bodies

& maybe when it leaks out through our eyes, the shine so bright y'all gotta squint to look

& maybe niggas don't like having to bow their eyelids to something bigger than their own ego

so these men stay / narrow-eyed and resentful / scared shitless / of all that light / in us.

A Woman Is Never Still

At one time,
if my nails had been painted
this shade of rose-foam, in Kabul
they would have rammed
out the frosted shell
like the tarp off
a bud's wet belly.
They would have gouged out
each shining beast
viscera still shiny,
each glittering pore
still insane
with breath.
The pain would have been meant
to shame me back to the realm
of several whitenesses;
they want to chew off
the cicatrix and lodge my
septic cadaver,
into a further gorge, where frisks
of neon riot in aporia,
where the humility
of the body is turned to iron

the shame is a
figure with an axe
climbing a voluting staircase,
it runs the speeding drams
with agility
from the hard pallet of the
radius to the soft roofs
of the mounds.
It famishes
the exquisitely nurtured
yellow
around which

breakers of scarp
hemorrhage
tigerish
glyphs, accomplishing
the gravity of
Japanese inscriptions.
A delicate cancer
bares its jaw;
tufts of blood
abound
in clay
sculpted
foetal knots,
a foetal navy,
they harden to seeds
crab-like, platinum,
growing beneath the
watery ceiling of the palm,
into amiable shoots;
an aubade on delphiniums
growing clearer each day.

Over many months
the permutations will again
show their round, maddening
faces,
the Persian inlay
will abound
with devout layers.
We will stroke on
the fine, sensual, nymphic
chemical
paint up to the ridges where we bleed the richest.
I cannot evade the force, brushing
further and further
iridescent texture
on my torso, spirit,
tongue
I'm a
bridge of veins
in air

I'm an orphic phantasm, hair
combed through with
stalactites.
I'm a bouquet
of limbs appliquéd
on pouring rain,
What can the spectral evening muster
in lament?

New Names for Brown Baby Girls

after Danez Smith

—bark of the old gum tree
—*Zulnoorain*
—palm creases wise with war
—first breath after three funerals
—war-drum in the distance
—allowed to cry above the burial ground
—reborn with the moon
—sworn ode to heaven
—*sukoon-e-sujood*
—rustle of dusk close to the sun
—juvenile pinky trying a vibrato on her first violin
—confidante
—pride
—never the burden, never unloved
—peak of the Lord's one-part-mercy
—last sob overcome, when you pray
—your only redemption
—*bulbul*, always ready to sing
—*Orooj-e-Zafar*
—ashless phoenix
—heart the size of a loosening fist
—unrippled surface of a mountain lake
—peace
—always peace

A Study of Anatomy, Although I Have No Desire to Study It

i. i never know what to with my hands, wrists twisting, fingers twitching. too often, they lie still, useless at my sides; too often, they have been told to be useful until they became a study in productivity, writhing snakes beside me, an antithesis of still life. the thing is, snakes cannot be controlled. they pounce, unpredictable, a betrayal of self. it is a terrifying thing when you live in a world where you only trust yourself with your mind—the knives and the butterflies and the ominous boom of your heart.

ii. it would be so easy to split myself in two: my mother's daughter and my father's, the barrier dotted in wired fence, crude and meanly built. i wonder if my indecision was borne of my duality, if i had always known on some subconscious level that i was a result of nuclear fusion rather than a whole being. no matter how obscure, how storm-hidden or sand-swept, the border remained. the no-man's-land that surrounded it was the blank-faced silence and the stuttered uncertainty of my answers when it came to my identity.

iii. alternatively, i was an ocean and my separate aspects of self were floating islands, their fates as precarious as that of atlantis. since evolution was a common enough occurrence in these parts, it was normal that these islands would pop up and disappear, their forests cut down and then rehabilitated. we are not constants, that's why people are flitting and flighty and often hurt others without meaning to because they can never control the waves or the weather.

iv. three months ago, my brother spread his mouth open, gaping, yawning, cavernous, and created a black hole in our living room—some irreparable chasm that sucked out whatever lovely feeling had been there before between us, and eventually it had swallowed him whole, too, a barbaric cannibalism that had overtaken the burning sun as it faded into the blinding white cold of winter (i wait for the summer to mend his soul).

v. a mother's heart is a rare collectible, a ceramic plate that her children throw against the floor, and relish the crash in their rebellion. our culture often prides itself on its sons who grow to be virtuous and strong and truly terrible, who often shatter the ceramic of their mother's heart, and learn to piece it together, then give it back like a dowry for her troubles. my mother does not say that our culture is a criminal that raises its sons to be killers.

vi. you are the only thing that does not reflect badly on my health, that does not dig its nails into the flesh underneath my eyes and scar it then colour it with a strong shade of insomnia. i see the years gather beneath my mother's eyes like rings in the bark of an aging tree, and i wonder who had planted the tree in the first place. i wonder if you had uprooted the trees growing in me.

Sidi Ali

My brother brought me kofta and fresh mangoes. He slept in the smallest apartment I've ever seen—a room, really, underneath the butcher's shop. I have forgotten his name. I brought him pants last summer. They fit him well. He smelled like fresh meat. He was sleeping when I first came to Salé, wouldn't wake up, not even for me. He calls our mother *Jamilah,* same as Meryam, same as me. He brought me a bracelet from the beggars by the mosque. He refused my money. We watched action movies together because through our many languages, violence is universal. When we broke our fast, I always ate first. We had nothing to say to each other. In the end, we had nothing to say to each other.

Gnawa Boy, Marrakesh, 1968

The maker has marked another boy to die:
his thin body between two sheets,
black legs jutting out onto the stone floor,
the tips of his toenails translucent as an eye.
Gray clumps of skin, powder-light,
like dust on the curve of his unwashed heel
and the face, swollen, expanding like a lung.
At its center, the sheet lifts and curves:
his body's strangeness, even there.
One palm faces down to show the black
surface of hand, the other facing up
white as his desert's sky.
                                        As if underwater,
he passes from that room into the blue
porcelain silence of the hall, where the light-
skinned women have gathered in waiting:
no song of final parting, no wailing
ripped holy from their throats:
the women do not walk into the sun,
they hide their bodies from it
(those pale wrists, those pale temples):
they do not walk the streets,
they do not clutch their own bodies,
they do not hit themselves in grief—

Haratin Girl, Marrakesh, 1968

—As the room is emptied of the boy's body
she watches through a hole carved into a wall of stone.
Quiet in the hall, the women carry the body awkwardly,
their pale hands tentative to touch it, grasping not the elbow or knee,
not the ankle or neck, but the rounded softnesses—
buttocks, side of torso—and the smallnesses—two fingers,
an ear, a tuft of rough hair—as if to carry him without touching him,
managing just enough to reach the end of the hall, where the girl
stares hard, her eyes strange and dark, then takes off running:
She does not begin the procession through the old city,
She does not pour the bathwater, or warm it, or salt it
(the neighbors will not come, the body cannot be cleaned):
She does not know why she rushes down the side street
to the small rooms where her mother and siblings sit, rushing
past the boys, already men, who spend each hour in waiting
of a nameless thing that will not come, past the small violence
they call to her in their lack, that violence she lets burn through her,
or run through her, dirty water through a deep bed of sand,
stopping to curse at them, or to pray for them, if not now for
the burning in her lungs, her lungs weak with swelling, swelling
with a fear so complete she will soon no longer know it as fear,
running into the medina, losing her shoes in the running,
the bottom of her feet bruising, toenails chipped, or chipping,
her face swollen, until, suddenly, she begins to slow her pace,
noticing the blue porcelain tiles and the marriage song ahead,
or to the west, her one good eye blinded, the mind scabbing around it,
beginning to understand somewhere inside herself, in a place she feels
but cannot name, or speak from, that she will for the rest of her life
run, even when her body does not run, even as she walks,
or sits, or carries the olive hand of a child, or children, not yet born—

Mother, *Ka'aba*

I moan and the nurse reminds me, *The Prophet said heaven is under the feet of mothers.*

When mothers give birth, the heaven under their feet is dark. *The first milk, called colostrum, isn't white*, she explains, places the pump on my breast.

*

Your mother then your mother then your mother then your father, said the Prophet, says the nurse. She insists I change the feminine pads regularly. Warm baths help.

*

The blood, the days—they don't stop. The pads irritate me. My husband gives me his white cotton undershirts to cut and use instead. Each shirt, a small offering. Each shirt, as white as milk, then dark.

*

The nurse tells me she missed her prayer rug after her first delivery. *Because we can't pray until the bleeding stops.* She peels the tape off my skin to remove the IV. She says mothers, too, are a kind of *Qiblah*, the direction in which we all pray in the end.

She presses her thumb into my arm. Mothers, a kind of *Ka'aba*. Removes the catheter. Final pilgrimage back to where we came from. Alcohol pad, gauze. Mothers, a first temple. Give thanks, circle seven times, counterclockwise. *Mabrook*, she smiles, *what a beautiful baby girl.*

Confession

Oh, I wish I had died before this and was in oblivion, forgotten.
—Mary giving birth, *The Holy Qur'an*

Truth be told, I like Mary a little better
when I imagine her like this, crouched
and cursing, a boy-God pushing on
her cervix (I like remembering
she had a cervix, her body ordinary
and so like mine), girl-sweat lacing
rivulets like veins in the sand,
her small hands on her knees
not doves but hands, gripping,
a palm pressed to her spine, fronds
whispering like voyeurs overhead—
(oh Mary, like a God, I too take pleasure
in knowing you were not all
holy, that ache could undo you
like a knot)—and, suffering,
I admire this girl who cared
for a moment not about God
or His plans but her own
distinct life, this fiercer Mary who'd disappear
if it saved her, who'd howl *to Hell*
with salvation if it meant this pain,
the blessed adolescent who squatted
indignant in a desert, bearing His child
like a secret she never wanted to hear.

Nakba Day Dance

attini a-nay wa ghani—
bring me the flute and
sing to me now, o sisters of my father—
i take shelter in the rose of damascus
ward a-shams, the taste of the language in my mouth like a meal—
how i could not cook the old recipes until i could say the words,
how more words came to me, in floods, in trickles,
links in a chain, twists in a rope
the twists in a silken thread
red on the brocade of a young girl's dress—
ayn al-bukara, the eye of the cow, the moon over bethlehem,
the windmill in long rows done by hand without a grid or guide or pattern,
the chicken's feet border, the roosters
on each shoulder, a lily for purity at the neck
where the thob opens, where the crocheted ties are with clover leaf at the end
the chevron and cedars of gaza like a necklace.

sing to me now, sisters of my sitti—
women i will never meet even in pictures or stories
my aunts and girl-cousins who would teach me the dances before weddings
at the party of the brides, women dancing together, cheering on women,
the memory sweet and fresh like a date in the desert of my mind.
here i am parched.
a refugee's talent is to make friends wherever she goes.
a refugee's fate is to keep wandering always, always making new friends,
always finding herself in someone else's home.
i apologize, i try to watch closely for the rules,
each house a new regime, each cohort of friends a new camp to survive.

sing to me now, mother of my heart
in your true voice so purely country and southern—
how you sang out so freely your few words of old speech, hayk filaheen
you cross the world to be a country woman again,
barefoot with a scarf on your hair.
find now a new life, one that is your own,

find your children in the very act of losing them
to history, to geography, to their own silvering hair.

sing to me now, so that wherever i pass,
i can thread my certainty on the sound of the family names,
the villages and farms where you knew trees and their individual personalities—
give me hope, fill me with strength to make one day a home
that will be my own. give me a window on the world
in which i can live and burn, a candle lit,
a message to all who pass this way, a song that sings:
come home. rest here. taste this. dance.
ghani. sing.

Ode to Dalya's Bald Spot

my sister wraps the throw
around herself on the small
cream loveseat & i know
for sure that she is not
a speck of dirt on a pill.
she coughs & sniffs up all
the lucky air in the room
into her excellent nostrils,
which are, endless
holy wells replenishing
the soft architecture of her guts.
not even the lupus can interrupt
this ritual of beholding.
you ever look at a thing
you ain't make, but, become
a mother in the looking?
our blood is a thread tied
around my finger, tied
around her finger, that helps
me love. when her knees
swell, when her joints rust,
when her hair thins & flees
making a small continent
of skin on the side of her head,
i am witnessing her in whatever
state her body will allow.
Bismillah to the brain that
put my name next to her name
and said *look at this girl your*
whole life and know some kind
of peace. littlest bald spot, that no one
expected or knew how to love
you remind me of us.
i know Dalya's thinking, *how ugly*
what a shame, but, i wanna
build a mosque right then

& there. make an annual
Haaj to that brown meadow.
slick as a coin. little planet
uncolonized. flagless.
her awful, but her own.

Hot Combs and Hijabs

How could I forget my mother,
her nails painted grapefruit red every week,
her trips to Nordstrom for a new pair
of open-toed heels, sling-backs, and wedges
that she matched perfectly with her hijabs?
How could I not recall her strutting
in the masjid in her diamond studded jeans?
Her love of Tresor perfume? My mother knew
how to keep herself together in this faith.
She taught me how to balance two worlds:
how to fry fish in steamy masjid kitchens
and where to place the wine glass and soup spoon
on a proper dinner table. She passed down
her mother's slips and camisoles, opera gloves
and mink stoles, turned Sunday hats
into Friday tams, switched between hot combs
and hijab pins, followed Arabic classes
with piano lessons by uncle Arthur.
How could I not remember how she posed
at the Peabody Club's Christmas brunch,
a glass of sparkling cider in one hand,
her Swarovski clutch in the other,
toe out, hip to the side,
then still *dhikred* after prayer that night?
She'd caravanned to Detroit and Atlanta,
those meccas of black Muslims,
but kept summers for grandparents in St. Louis
where she braided and beaded my hair,
let me run free and never apologized
for the freedom of conversion.

Tapestry

I.
Your father wasn't born the same way as us,
said my cousins. I asked, *how then?* And they
told me grandfather split open bamboo,
found a crying babe in its hollow.

No, that's someone else! said one cousin.
Uncle was found inside the biggest coconut fruit—
there are suddenly voices flying, my cousins
giving different versions of one thing.

I believed them.

II.
Mother said grandfather left her and grandmother because the local river was too wide for grandmother to cross and too narrow for grandfather to wade through. Mother found grandfather years after grandmother left behind ashes and when he came to our house I was scared because the blood is the same yet the song is not, so I became a little ghoul in lightless corners.

Grandfather left us a year later. Mother knew when she woke up to the smell of his favorite cologne. I expected the sky to share mother's grief—instead, both our throats burned and our eyes were dry pools.

III.
You do not remember the house you grew up in.
What you do remember is the cousin who lives there
with her girlfriend and the girlfriend's family for
whom your cousin works. Father tells you
your cousin is held at sword-point, gun-point.
Your uncle tells you she has become a ghost.

You do not tell them
the house is the ghost.

Loving All My Mothers / a DNA Joy in Hachi Hullo Li (i love you)

i know Great Granny Lily's people got miles on their soles.
conceived on appropriated land that her folx did not reserve for themselves.
her young body sold for $50. took her straight off the Oklahoma reservation.
she was menstrual flow fresh. Never consulted, no consent.
raised her only baby alone.

Lily knew about these moon cycles.

i know Granny Dorothy constructed us rituals.
rolled her own smokes. taught herself to read.
didn't speak much about Lily except for blackberries & sugar.
dominoes. cornbread & stovetop bacon grease.
sat grandchildren down in dirt to sweat it out.
would get a switch and threaten her greats about "getting some gratitude."
didn't care for no man. pointed her only child's baby daddy out just once.
some "half breed" passing through on business.
Granny raised that lil girl alone too.

Dorothy know about them moon cycles.

Grandma Jean.
some say you look at her and she catch it.
married young. many times before i met my Papaw.
tells me she did it to get away.
pushed out all them babies young too. just like womb moons before.
first one right there on Lily's kitchen floor.

Says it was no kind of Indian magic. no tobacco smoke lifting prayers.
no placenta placed back into earth. Not the way tv or them books tell it.
Dorothy tell her "hush all that hollering up, you wouldn't making all that noise when you made them babies."
Jean know Lily & Dorothy wanted to go back to the rez.
i know they never did.
i wonder if they'd of took all that raw talk back too.

Jean know about a cycle. a moon.

Moms got bitter in her lineage. menstral flow fresh never consulted, no consent.
a man she wished she'd never known as daddy.
i know she got tumultuous tongue twisted in tradition. i know.
Moms know about a cycle. a moon.

just me. don't know my genetic daddy. not at all. i bear witness. about a cycle.
  a moon destined to split.
if I could speak of DNA joy. even in fragments. i might let the moon know.
Hachi Hullo Li (i love u).

Unmotioning

Especially in line for the food bank,
my mother radiated grace. Talked
a machinery of Principles. Elm trees
and their dresses of urine, her small mouth
always chiding, don't speak to a man of that kind.
This daily commitment to life felt laborious, haram.
Expendable it was, like all my milk teeth
knocked back into my mouth. That taste.
What even is sustenance? She was a woman of Principles,
she flossed, her exquisite fangs displaying remorse
only when she reprimanded me or talked of the coat.
Consider the white lab coat hanging
above a crusted heater; consider our dilapidating shame.
Consider me. Tonight, I exercise humility,
So, I identify with the pigeons
gnawing on the chicken wing grey as the sky.
Unparagraphed I am, the way I still steal
my dinner from a health store on 6th Ave.,
then lecture the diorama with my lentil soup.
The truth is, I never educated myself
the way I cultivated my limits.
I was an abandoned thought,
marching through an unlocked window—
I had an albino budgie once, red ink for eyes.
He wore a lab coat and crashed against my window
like a displaced insect. His name was Apollo. Some circumstances never abandon
you, you only train the muscle that carries them.
Is a wing a muscle? *3 Best Exercises for Building Badass Wings*,
says the ad, and the man in the subway
sprawled across hard plastic looks like
a glorious bone. In his odor, I feel at home.
Consider his careful dedication to repose.
There is something he has mastered genuinely,
his fist curled around it. Sleeps on two cushions,
one for his ass. She was a woman of Principles.

Consider her stark god of oblivion.
Nobody would've differentiated between us and him.
Uniformly standing in line, a dark puff, plume on the wing.
The wing patched to the torso of a body entirely ignorant of aerodynamics.
The world hadn't hurt us more than
it had hurt anyone else, but still, I couldn't trust the sky
and its reverberations. In line, I made friends with a family
of crickets in white lab coats. They sang to me,
of the end of it, that wings were awaiting us there:
stale bread rolls, a cheese pie,
Braeburn apples sharing space
with two cans of tomatoes.

Smell Is the Last Memory to Go

on my block, a gate
on my block, a tree smelling

of citrus & jasmine that knocks
me back into the arms of my dead

mother. i ask Ross *how can a tree*
be both jasmine & orange, on my block

my neighbors put up gates & stare
don't like to share, on my block

a tree I can't see, but can smell
a tree that can't be both but is

on my block, my mother's skirt twirls
& all i smell is her ghost, perfume

on my block, a fallen orange
smashed into sidewalk

it's blood pulped on asphalt on my
block, Jordan hands me a jasmine

by the time i get home
all it's petals are gone

The Woman in the White Chador

stands on the flat roof of a house in Masuleh.
She left lunch on the stove to walk out

on the layer cake of terraced houses on the hillside,
one row above the other, roofs turning into roads below.

She is not an idea.
Erect, draped, one arm crosses

the bright white of her chest
to hold the swath in place.

Leucistic bird: occurrence.
The windows below her are wide open.

The fog rolls up the hill below us,
peers over our shoulders and into all the houses

as if to move us inside.
She could call us to prayer and I would.

She was born where I wasn't.
She is so white she shines

through the muck of others' disbelief.
The day stays foggy.

She is not an idea, and I didn't
put her there. She's not there to jump.

She's there to say she did not jump.

Sacraments

I kiss my shoulders, right first,
stretch great-winged.
I turn and he's not there.
I'm not at his right.
The thread between us
is certainly metallic,
sensitive to vibration.
I submit to them,
and he's not present.
Other men speak to me
in the language of devotion
until he's a man again.

While I'm inventing gods,
why don't I build an altar:
a brick-littered fire escape.
Even the wall supporting
my altar makes offerings.
The birds and flies make none
I can find. I'd only accept
one from the swallow perched
with its mouth open
before it flew. I wait
for my congregation.
The swallow left a berry
on the banister, pared
and scattered to ash.

Our sacrament requires wet wipes,
for sensitive skin,
from an aisle concerned
with preserving new skin,
encouraging sleep.
This seems holy.

I'd also consider a bag of keys

or buttons.
It's better to worry a wet wipe.
It's nice to worry something fresh.
I invite my congregants
to scrub their necks, say:
My wedding day was unremarkable.
Run a sheet under breasts, say:
It's a lover's job to examine me.
In the absence of one,
I ask cells to behave.
Remove dried eyeliner
from an otherwise clean face,
say: I like men best
when they don't know,
so ask whether to test
approach with finger,
tongue, member.
A last dripping wipe
under toenails, say: I've always
wanted to be in a headlock
so I can bite the crook
of an arm, tear.
I bless elbows after needing
friends to turn my doorknobs.

Then we wait until sunset, watch
a window go bright. A naked torso
behind raised blinds,
a hand lifting the window.

I tell them we allow despair
until the next train passes.
These weeks, they cross each other,
giving us more time.
We listen to kids scream
as trains pass overhead.
If we close our eyes,
it's an amusement park.
Children whistle under the tracks.
Not songs. Actual whistles:

curt blows as rubber soles
toe lines and don't cross them.
Race away.
They also practice
a victim's screams:
whoever sounds best murdered,
wins applause. Who ever practiced
screaming like the killer?

After the Orlando Shooting

On being of the same origin as both the victim and the shooter

I.

I've had this dream before,
the one in which I am naked
and wear a necklace of bullets
and drag my dead body,
also naked and full of stones.

II. *To My Dead Body*

The night of your neck
carries bolts of lightning,
that cackle through you.
The night of your back
is full of exit wounds
the color of stars.

I hold you,
and light bleeds through my fingertips.

The night of your night is beautiful.

The night belongs to you.

I am sorry.

III. *The First Time I Made Love to a Man*

It was Summer,
and clouds thinned themselves across the sky.
After we finished
I thought the sky would fill itself with stones.
Instead, the day continued on as it would.

IV.

I've had this dream before,
the one in which I am naked
and wear a necklace of bullets
and drag my dead body,
also naked and full of stones.

I am so close to death.

I listen to it
and hear myself.

My body will never be remembered.

Anneanne Tells Me

i miss my friends. they are all dead now. hopefully one day you will know what the moon feels like in your hands. that's how it felt to first hold you. *benim aşkim.* remember my old home & the ghosts between the floorboards? i miss them. i miss your small knees, always scraped.

lütfen, beyza, call me when you get home.

III.

HAJJ

Our Mothers Fed Us Well

after Katherine Liu

The story begins and ends here, a mouth unopen, the girl buried as she is born. The sky heaving, stars unlit. A man spills god in the humid air and they all bow their heads. Ameen. Piece by piece, the building crumbles, the stone rots. The little mosque at the end of the road, midnight, with her sister and her sister's children. Even here, she does not fit. Even here, she is a stranger. The hard cost of English, tongue betraying the skin. All the women and children clustered together like bad teeth. I don't mean to make a habit of these things, but somehow, loss trails me, the people I touch turned to stone. Midnight, in the little apartment, the city and its lovers sleeping, even the stray dogs quiet, even the begging women and their empty mouths gone.

Freedom Bar

I wear the hijab and walk into Freedom Bar.
Someone says *Go home terrorist!* and I wake up
in my kitchen with my mother worrying about
changing my brother's name, *Osama*, she peels
a wooden onion, *It means lion in Arabic.* Tears
stream down her face and their liquid salt
fills my mouth.

I walk into Freedom Bar, the bartender looks
at me suspicious, a red bowtie glints below his mane
when he flips a bottle with his tail. I chug the "Home
Sweet Home" and wake up undressed in Old
Persia in the royal calligrapher's bed. He licks his qalam
and glides strokes of soot and Arabic gum
on my thighs.

Avval valî uftâd mushkilhâ, Hafez hums
on the stool next to mine. He slides a gold coin
into the jukebox that lights up to Fairuz's voice, *Take me
and plant me in the land of Lebanon. What* were *you
doing in Lebanon, ma'am?* I stand naked at Kennedy
Airport, x-rays miss the bullet in my tongue, security
looks for visa stamps.

I wake up on the kitchen table, mother stirring
olive stones in the wok, *Will he ever come back?*
she cries over the phone. *I'm looking!* I yell back
in the silence of the drones in the fields of Waziristan
where I watch farmers water Muhammad's names
around mud houses for protection. *Peace Be Upon Him,*
they say, *Take this home.*

I carry the "Inshallah" pickled in water and circle
the Ka'aba when someone says *Woman, go home!
God forbids you to enter His house without a man.*
I wake up on the kitchen floor, mother boiling

his T-shirts with pages of the Qu'ran, *Go tell him*
I've made his favorite soup. I wear the hijab
and walk into Freedom Bar.

Snake Oil, Snake Bite

They staunched the wound with a stone.
They drew blue venom from his blood
        until there was none.
When his veins ran true his face remained
lifeless and all the mothers of the village
wept and pounded their chests until the sky
        had little choice
but to grant their supplications. God made
        the boy breathe again.

God breathes life into us, it is said,
only once. But this case was an exception.
God drew back in a giant gust and blew life into the boy
and like a stranded fish, he shuddered, oceanless.

It was true: the boy lived.
He lived for a very long time. The toxins
were an oil slick: contaminated, cleaned.
But just as soon as the women
kissed redness back into his cheeks
the boy began to die again.
He continued to die for the rest of his life.
The dying took place slowly, sweetly.
The dying took a very long time.

Morning Prayer in Taino Warpaint

Tainos are pomegranates.
          Brown in rotting,
they call me inverted apple.
Woman with bowl of bija: for your skin
it restores all of the red
fucked out of this island.

This island
once faced the sky like a pomegranate
cut in half, clusters of red.
If it weren't for your rotting
                              skin,
your red parts wouldn't be an apple.

You bruise like an apple,
too, not like the body of this island.
There are parts of your skin
bija cannot restore. The parts that aren't pomegranates.
The brown parts. The rotting
is what she calls the brown parts, as she paints red

all over my body. How the red
comes to my skin like an open wound. Apple
of Eden. I am rotting
golden in the throat of this island,
golden in the husk of the pomegranate
golden in the bruised skin

and golden in the unbruised skin.
How the white man wishes to hang us red,
God, they want to hang me on a pomegranate
tree and gut me like an apple.
Make me forbidden on my own island
and all of its rotting.

Here, branches hold onto forgotten fruit. Dear rotting
God, forgive me for coming to you in this dyed skin,
But I have returned my limbs to this island.
Asked the woman with bija to dye them red.
God of gospel, I ask you to swallow me like a golden apple
or strange hanging pomegranate.

So that then, maybe you will ripen: the pomegranates, the rotting
body of apples caught in a white country's teeth, and the peeling skin
of the red, the slow beating muscle of this forgotten island.

Elegy

To lose a homeland you must give away
your stories. No sentences can be saved.

Verbs will break, abstract nouns will collapse and
precious centuries will wither away.

The world you spoke of and the world that spoke of you
will be caked in mud, strafed with smoke. You burn

the documents that will not pass checkpoints, the line
of refugees thickens, the siege aimed at

your ribcage sharpens its knives. You no longer want.
No possessions at this moment, no hunger for

a morsel of bread. Only a border passage.
Only the frayed hem of the horizon.

To lose a homeland you must give away your self.
Your words must break open, become empty

containers the shapes of which will forever
remind you of what you used to hold

inside   out beyond the greening fields
there is an old road to walk and it is

never paved it is never the place you used to
travel to in the lemon blossom dreams

you used to have when you owned a pillow or a
lantern or the solace of a language.

Saaro Umar

Geography Test

the archivist enters the room
with a bag of oranges

she
broke one on the walk over
her shirt tucked under bra strings
of juice
draw down her chin

he
is sitting at the table when she enters
facing the open window that
exits to
a skyline
licked with fog a thick cover of

buildings hang from the clouds

she hasn't yet learnt
to know words &
not their meaning

camera
spills
through the gaps in her teeth
lands within the hollow
that turns to plump
breast;
meeting place

her father walks to the kitchen sink
empties the steaming jug into terra cotta bowl
steeps the dried khat
until it turns to tea

they say the leaf of God
conjures old ghosts
but he weathers the nightmares
for the memories

the children
marching in two's past
where he stood cutting leaf & cane

the eldest of twelve
first from his village to
go to university
swallowed the language
of three colonizers

afaan oromo he
kept
hidden in the secret of his cheeks

she thought
everything unknowable stayed
hallowed in transit

the crackle of scalded onions
& oil
her aunty covered in gold & satin
towering over gleaming blue
hands filled
with wood & metal

as the doctor
eased her knees open
back pressed against
white linen
imitation cotton
forced against her meat

she found
etched onto
ceiling

two mountains
estranged by
migrant ash white
like the dripped
seed of the poplar in spring
clotted between the
blackened roots
of Odaa Nabee
the sound of thunder
kindling the floodplain;
meeting place

he takes his seat
at the table
an old study desk from
the salvo's reads like an atlas

scrunches a piece of green
places it in his mouth

rests his hands at the end of the counter
&
asks

where is your country?

she draws her
finger to the
middle of her chest
etching circles onto
skin

her tongue loops
the enclave of her cheeks

drawing rings
across flesh then slips
past the white threads
that drip from teeth

she gestures to the back of her
mouth her left palm remains
on breast

& says
in here

Common Ancestors

Echolalia. In the center of the shipwreck, there.
There the invention of one's own body. There the heliotropism

of something stalking east to west, a boat slicing its own shadow.
I play this immigration like a viola. If I forget Arabic,

then extinct is my grandmother, her lentil soup, the photographs water-
mottled, on the back الشام scrawled, and the year.

My last day in Beirut. Gridlock like a metal snake. An ex
posing for my camera, a wine bottle behind him.

It will be knocked over in five minutes. His eyes are shut,
teeth gritted. In this foxhole I was born twice:

hard and sober, steel piercing nose/lips/belly,
voodoo I stole from a darker woman. When I came to America,

white men took me to their mothers. I became proof,
mute and pretty. Spare underwear in my pocket like a firearm.

When anyone wanted to sink the day,
they called me first. Even the hospital gown had a lace collar.

I forgot that Zaynab came before Fatima. I drank on the first day of Eid.
From roof to dirt, say hallelujah, say hallelujah:

I'm a convert now. I'm a land waiting for my new, westerly name.

Ghazal

It's wine I need. Is it a sin to have another?
No harm in merlot, no harm in another.

In Ramadan, we'll break our fast with dates and wine—
Must we pray in one room and dance in another?

Crushed blossoms at the end of the summer: teach me
how to coax nectar from the bloom of another.

Burned rice on the stove again: what's to love
but my imperfections—you'll forgive me another.

Butter by a kettle always melts, warns the proverb.
Heated, greased, we slip one into the other.

When, inexplicably, you enter my prayers,
I hear messages from one god or another.

Me encanta cantar, cuando estoy sola, en el carro.
My mother tongue dissolves. I speak in another.

Heart-thief, enter the fields like a woman in love,
vase in one hand, shears in the other.

Washee / Was She

she was *washee* i told her you are
like your motherland a wilderness
needs a belt laid down two white
hotel towels took her into the tub to
wuzu the boys out of her mouth pointed
her nipples toward qibla wiped clean
her intention to perform *ruk'u* as if
carrying a glass of chai on her back
fold at the knees palms to the ground
tucked her soles under her *astaghfirullah*
used country

in my used country I felt his teeth
circle as a mosquito the black mystery
he placed my *right* hand over my wrong
stain said he was bringing me *home*
offered me a suite with a lock a key in
the shape of a *brother* perhaps twenty-
two years old my body pure as a glass
table he spilled *was she* my boss on my
back at night came easy as a fly
to post-conflict *faithfully*
used my country

Human

When my parents call they ask me to come
back. Their voices crackle over thousands of
miles when my mother tells me she misses me and my
father tells me he knows a firm I should apply to. I'm casting
a wide net for my job hunt, sure, but I've only been
catching butterflies; in this landscape neither I nor
the butterflies are secure. With an insect fanning
my blushing face, a white noise machine, I move my
mouth in shapes that indicate I might come back. The
truth is I'm gone to some violent air, there are no
eyes here, just whirling. It's like I was thrown onto
the ground belly-down and my wings were torn
off and pinned to the wall. It's gross and beautiful.
For some reason the only brother I haven't come out
to has convinced my parents I should look for work in
busier places, I suppose he knows. But then
again, he's never been tactful, he'd take a gun
instead of a net and snipe the impossible for fun.
Work-work-work, he would say, clutching an Ayn
Rand book between his teeth. God. She didn't
think much of people like us except in
terms of destruction and
genocide. Destruction and
genocide. What kind of
storm are we facing where
getting wiped our for being born
feels inevitable? Listen, every newspaper
contains my obituary. I suppose I could stay
and defeat deportation; I'll hide between this
paper that says my people should be shot and
this paper that says my people should be bombed
and this paper that says I'm continuing my
education by working at a firm. Every day is the hot
mark of a brand. Look, I'm really scared. How many
blame me, expect an apology, find me an invasive
species? How can we turn back from the fascist
disaster, the fear of being, the paranoid battle with
being deleted? I could scream. I don't know how to
dodge, like I'm the cherry tree to Washington's
axe. I could turn back now, and live with a less
virulent fear, but I've come too far now to let the
storm steal my skin. When I told my friend I
didn't know where I would end up she told me to
bite the bullet.

Bilal Al-Shams

sacrifice

my father taught me to kill gentle.
        to use the small blade.
no need for extravagance.
        there is one job to be done.

the children must be fed.
        the lamb is what we have to offer.
i am nineteen. i am a boy
        who longs to be a man.

all it takes is one motion.
        a small cut, my father says. *the throat*
is the softest place on any animal.
        abu ali ties its feet together.

i grip the dagger's handle.
        bismillah al-rahman al-rahim.
hesitate. close my eyes. relinquish all guilt.
        for us to eat, something must die.

today, i hold a different blade. machete.
        two feet of ungodly metal.
there is a place that will sharpen my sword for cheap.
        the sound of the machine the most prayerful hum.

i wait, cross-legged. wonder when
        i will have to choose my life or another's.
i am a few weeks fresh from the latest hate crime.
        i am still shaking from the memory

of everyone watching, no one trying to help.
        i am a man who longs to be a boy again.
i know too much of the world and its people.
        how they decide who deserves to be spared.

but my father raised me

to never make the same mistake twice.
all it takes is one motion.
a small cut. any part of the body

is soft when the steel is jagged enough.
i keep the weapon between the two front seats
of my nissan. i will never let a white man
come at me like that again.

when i have nightmares
i say the holy words.
bismillah al-rahman al-rahim.
in the name of god, the most gracious and merciful.

i am both
the sacrificial lamb and the executioner.
the scapegoat and the swordslayer.
the one screaming and the angel of death.

all blades
are made of metal.
chromium, manganese, vanadium
titanium, copper, damascus steel

all metal is torn from the earth
melted, and reshaped into a weapon.
this weapon, the only thing
keeping me from returning to the soil.

but i know
the limitations of my self-defense.
a muslim boy with a sword
is empty compared to a white man with a gun.

but what is a god to a non-believer.
if i am to be the sacrifice, i will stain the ground
with everything irreplaceable.
we fight

even the deadliest plague.

i blink and i am nineteen again.
sabre in hand. i hesitate. close my eyes.
mouth full of guilt. i do not know how to kill

but there is nothing that cannot be taught.
perhaps my father meant this to be training.
or maybe all he wanted
was for us to eat in peace.

bismillah. bismillah. bismillah.
i pull the knife like a thread.
the lamb's blood
the same color as mine.

Relinquish

I did climb up that mountain and wash my hair with snow
I did not leave my regrets there wedged between schist and sage brush
Before I left the house I did put the limp celery in a glass of water
I did not strip naked when I went into the mountain lake

I did go in so quickly my heart clenched up
I could not unclench it afterward, not even when seized
By my old vertigo as the funicular car dipped and it seemed
We were plummeting straight into the rocks

Not the first time I fell from height, there was that time my fingers
Slipped on a bar as I was reaching up and I fell six feet flat on my back
If I close my eyes tight I can still summon up the flower of pain
Spiking out the back of my head

For a minute I thought I was dead and then for two more I thought
"I am alive? But I forget what that means"
Stumbled like a ghost through a building whose edges seemed to quiver
Same as the funicular cables bearing us creepily down

Elliot climbed up with us but hiked back down,
he did not want to get into that steel sky-stabbed car
I can't soar, I haven't learned very much in my life, I've just become a better
   fuck-up
And I turned 45 this year, aren't I supposed to know something about something?

Nah says the mountain with that classic stony expression
I did learn to play cards with my cousins when I was very young
I did not ever let them win
I did finally toughen up into a little skinny beast

I did not give up my attraction to having nocturnal eyes, flower lips and
   medusa hair
I did eat the celery stalks when I came back, a little sun-dazed, a little cloud-
   proud

I did not drink enough water and so spent all evening trying to speak in tongues
What possible prayer can we offer to return to a place that shows us death

Where a body can unfold the overheard bars of the sky so fully unseen
And clamber across the night hand over hand on starry rungs
A bell rings somewhere in the distance, neither church nor klaxon alarm
Still lake-shocked, I did try to invent an excuse to stay

Having collected June snow in my old familiar hands
But coldness and scratches on my arms and legs remind me of who I am
I do now risk my wind-tossed fate on a last dangerous gambit
Pursuant to that most rare clause of the bedrock's odd contract I stake no claim

My Imminent Demise Makes the Headlines the Same Day I Notice How Even Your Front Teeth Are

At the internment camp, promise me you'll take the top bunk.
I want to see you every time I look up.
National anthems are still more violent than most hip hop lyrics.
Sugar-coat me this. I know.
Got a sense of humour blacker than my granddaddy's knuckles.
You are the sinkhole into which I pour my desperations.
My sixth pillar. Validate me, if only with the soft explosions
of your breath. Its daily, naked persistence.
Who cares if they burn our houses?
Our bones?
Yes. We might lose our reflections.
We might lose our names.
We might lose feeling in both hands.
Our blood will still dry solid. Still keep its colour. A kind of Abrahamic love
to outlast the mist of rain,
the depth of waters,
the permanence of chicken grease on fingers.
Find me a world as eternal as the birthmark between your shoulders.
Find me a sign as prophetic as a boy born with a target on his back.
Haven't you heard?
Every time my thighs rub together,
God answers a prayer.
This heart is not a footrest.
For you,
I can make an exception.
We can make a life out of such exceptions.

Habeshawit

My grandfather's skin smelled like civil war and birbire. He used to call me Ethiopia. Between kissing both of my cheeks, he'd tell me (as a message to my mother) that should've been my birth name.

I don't speak Amharic. I piece together the meanings of questions distant relatives ask. I squint my eyes and smile. They always call me konjo. That means I'm pretty. I answer them in English. They pity my tongue like a lost cause.

I live in a place I've not made a home of. I was born here. I don't know what to tell people when they ask me where I'm from. I don't know what it means when they ask me what I am. I'm of a place I've not actually been to. Home is where I say it is. I have to say something. Black people say black people don't look like me. I'm black. I have spiraling hair and big eyes and a red glow during the summer months. My blood is hot and longing.

I feel most at home while in transit (to anywhere).

I'm a visitor in my own bedroom.

I'm the village beauty of a ghost town.

Ars Poetica

Autobiography practiced in the enemy's language has the texture of fiction.
—Assia Djebar, *Fantasia*

in ohio i tell a classroom of white students a story i mean to be beautiful
about my grandfather   retreating in his old age to his first tongue

in which there are no separate words for *like* & *love*   once at a restaurant
meaning   i think   to say *i would like some tomato soup*   repeats

to our flustered waitress   *i love tomato soup*   *i love tomato soup*
& the white students & the white professors like my story   they think i
mean it

to be comic   the room balloons with their delight   they are laughing
at my grandfather & it is my fault   for carving tendernesses from my old life

without context   parading to strangers my weak translations
now they think i am joking & lap   at my every dripping word

& isn't this why i learned this language   to graduate
from my thick & pungent newness   my accent & my nameless shoes   to float

my hands like a conductor   redirect the laughter to a body not my own
for a moment of quiet inside my traitor's head

How to Say

algebra becomes Ali-Jebrah   becomes
or   i thought i was using the right accent

becomes   i say it right   mama speak Arabic
when she become inter-prey-tar   becomes

Mustafa Al Sunni through the car   because
the radio is haram sometimes   becomes

how would he say it   when doing his equations
at the kitchen table   becomes how would he say

it down the pub with the boys   becomes how would
he say it   crushing pomegranate to his teeth

Accent

You think while drinking Arabic coffee,
at the house of your Saudi friends,
that you have been embraced,
that they don't see your black skin.

You think of how you've helped them
revise their essays for their business classes
at IU, how you've taught them
what a Hoosier is and how to pronounce
the word *cousin* with an s, not a z
like you say with your family in Memphis.

You think of how you spoke up for them
after 9/11. So, you're confused when they snicker
after you ask, *What time is prayer at the masjid*?
They remind you it's *mahs-jid,* not *maas-jid.*
You thank them for their lesson
and think of how everyone back home
spoke like you spoke.

You wonder what other Arabic words
you speak come out black,
how your *As-Salaam Alaikum*
sounds more like *Slam-lakum,*
how you pronounce the Arabic letter *ain*
like *ain't,* as in *There ain't nothing*
I can't do as good as you.

You always held your breath
when your 11th grade English teacher,
Mrs. Mulherin, called students to read
out loud. Each time she made you stand
and face the class when you said *aks*
rather than *ask.* You learned
to switch tongues
around your cousins,

that it was ok to say, *I ain't tell nobody.*
But you'd always say *Bismillah*
under your breath
as they said *Amen*
during grace at Sunday dinners.
You wonder how many times
you've translated yourself.

Last New Year's Eve, you opened your home
to your friends, spent hours
making a playlist of '90s R&B songs
only to have your Palestinian friend
turn off your music because it was *haram.*
You wondered whether you were in your own house
or his.

Even now, sitting in line for prayer,
you avoid calling the *adhan*. You remember
what your Saudi friends said:
You can only know God in Arabic.
Your remember what your voice carries—
your long drawl, your black-eyed peas
and collard greens, your parents' Christianity.
It reveals your black neck, your familial
disconnect, your fried chicken breath.

Reporting Live from Hookah Lounge

after Safia Elhillo

what is home but two
loose teeth that won't fall

i can nudge
with my clunky tongue

never hold
why can't i feel the tides

between their bodies   mine & which
earth   body will claim my mouth

tonight

i will breathe the ocean
of smoke over pages of

my notebook   my skirt
i want to leave here

smelling like *double apple*
mint & lemon   tea

and sugar   perfumed
like a black fairuz

but this room pronounces
its throbbing heart   *qalbi*

so maybe i'll leave this place
more like umm kulthum

body passed down
from hand to hand

a miles-long funeral's
embrace a black body/

a brown body. so impossibly
far   from home

Burden of Proof

After the towers, I never left
an empty grocery cart astray

but rolled it across the parking lot
back to its designated spot.

On the road, I signaled right
and left with every change of lane,

nodded, *thank you, sorry,*
please, not a problem.

I pinned ribbons—yellow, pink,
red—on T-shirts and hijabs,

organized drives—blood,
toys, canned foods.

And when a stranger's eyes
groped my bags at the terminal,

I smiled and suffocated
the dynamite in my chest.

Farah Ghafoor

Oxygen

After the Peshawar school massacre, December 2014

The day is in full yawn
The day is a mouth that the boys jump
into, their foul mouths cursing
The day is a panting plume of dust above their nicest
shoes, above their cricket bats that glow
with sweat when their mothers sweep them
inside, their faces knotted in a *du'a* or curse
The day had *raat ki raani* breath, sweet and fervent
enough to pull at their kites strings as they bit
into the boys' palms like blades
The day had a tongue that rang a school bell
and they yearned for its dry lips to press together
and kiss their foreheads before bed

The day is in full yawn
which mean the brain needs oxygen
and not a tongue like a gun and not a school bus
to be a yellow bullet
The day is a mouth until it is crushed
by men who want to measure life in dominoes, in boys
who fall one by one still in their uniforms
The day is a panting body dragging itself back to
its friend to lay in his blood, to play pretend
for the last time and to show teeth intact
The day had breath scented of night-blooming
wounds, how they would open unwittingly to darkness
The day had a tongue that rang a siren
that came to kiss the boys asleep.

I am in full yawn
My mouth is a habit of curtains drawing
themselves together, of huddling under the white sheets
and of covering the chests that shutter silent.
My mouth is a panting imam after he calls

again *Inna lillahi wa inna ilayhi raji'un—*
to Allah we belong and to Him is our return—*Inna lillahi*
wa inna ilayhi raji'un into the dirt
My breath is scented of skin, paper, the number
of seconds in a school day
My tongue is the scream of a sun
of boys being buried under the horizon

The day is in full yawn
and I am always in need of oxygen

Gerisi, Eylül / Rest, Eylül

Bugün benim en güzel günim. Çok mutluyum. Bugün benim için başka güzel bir gün olacak . . . ben artik yapamiyorum.

Today is my most beautiful day. I'm so happy. Today is going to be another beautiful day for me . . . I can't do this anymore.

—The first few words of Eylül Cansın's suicide note, recorded before she jumped off the Bosphorus Bridge in Istanbul.

onu son birkaç kelime
annesi vardı
o olabilir soran
köpeğini ilgileneceğim.
Lütfen, beni düşün
ona bakmak zaman.
Sadece beni düşün.
& onu vermeyin
kimseye.

(her last few words
were to her mother
asking if she could
take care of her dog.
Please, think of me
whenever you look at her.
Think of only me.
& don't give her away
to anyone.)

Things Get Harder When It Rains

a moon filled with silver rings sits next to me & asks how i'm feeling.

the same moon begins to get honest with me in a way that i have never experienced a moon to be honest. a lot of the time, moons tend to lie to me. i tend to love them anyway. but this moon is different & she is something like a wheel, always moving wherever people tell her to.

this is where we are supposed to discuss magic but when are we not discussing magic in the ways we fuck, or the ways we disappoint, as if those are two different things?

this moon doesn't remember the first night she met me & i understand.
there were so many other things going on, but for some reason i couldn't forget it.
the lake was there, laughing as always. her ripples wouldn't stop shaking her surface
& all the moon could do was reflect. it was spring
& there were still christmas lights hanging from houses hidden in the trees.

this moon peels off a few rocks from her skin & we skip them until the lake breaks down crying. we run.

i think about suicide & who would feed the dog i never really owned.

i think about my constant heartache & picture driving on the highway for the first time.

Midnight in the Foreign Food Aisle

Dear Uncle, is everything you love foreign
or are you foreign to everything you love?
We're all animals and the body wants what it wants,
I know. The blonde said *Come in, take off*
your coat and *what do you want to drink?*
Love is not haram but after years of fucking
women who cannot pronounce your name,
you find yourself in the foreign food aisle,
beside the turmeric and the saffron,
pressing your face into the ground, praying
in a language you haven't used in years.

Dias/phoria Suite

Some nights/My body
feels like this foreign country
my visa expired

lines drawn across skin
written on bodies/Given
accident status

soft bush guards inter-
stice granting asylum from
belonging/Or worse

press your hands wanting
shelter in displacement kiss
honey thighed exile/

beyza ozer

Hello, This Letter Was Never Finished

this is where i would draw a map & title it *the place for ache*

a black hole disguised as heaven, or

maybe not even disguised, maybe it's just a portal

    this is how i pray: think about my hands

    & how they look older than the rest of me

    there are no differences between warm mornings

    & apologies that end with flowers in the trash

i could make a blanket for someone but i'd rather

sit on a roof & pretend to look for meteors

when the sun pushes out you will still find me there

i'm not scared of floods anymore

    & asking for forgiveness is so difficult

    i forgot how to say so many words in my first language

    but i am practicing by reading eulogies

    whose idea was it to keep distance?

my eyes are about to give out again but

here, take this dynamite for when i wake up

If They Come for Us

these are my people & I find
them on the street & shadow
through any wild all wild
my people my people
a dance of strangers in my blood
the old woman's sari dissolving to wind
bindi a new moon on her forehead
I claim her my kin & sew
the star of her to my breast
the toddler dangling from stroller
hair a fountain of dandelion seed
at the bakery I claim them too
the Sikh uncle at the airport
who apologizes for the pat
down the Muslim man who abandons
his car at the traffic light drops
to his knees at the call of the Azan
& the Muslim man who drinks
good whiskey at the start of maghrib
the lone khala at the park
pairing her kurta with crocs
my people my people I can't be lost
when I see you my compass
is brown & gold & blood
my compass a Muslim teenager
snapback & high-tops gracing
the subway platform
Mashallah I claim them all
my country is made
in my people's image
if they come for you they
come for me too in the dead
of winter a flock of
aunties step out on the sand
their dupattas turn to ocean
a colony of uncles grind their palms

& a thousand jasmines bell the air
my people I follow you like constellations
we hear glass smashing the street
& the nights opening dark
our names this country's wood
for the fire my people my people
the long years we've survived the long
years yet to come I see you map
my sky the light your lantern long
ahead & I follow I follow

IV.

SALAH

I've Watched Myself Die Twice This Week

41 times in Istanbul, 49 in Orlando.

I'm not sure where these parts of my old body

end & where soil begins. Not sure where the soil

begins & ends at the edge of an ocean. Any ocean.

Pick any fucking ocean. I am waiting for all 5 of them

to pull me apart. Better them than any human. Better

them than a fear of walking outside. Going to a club.

An airport. I just want to live again. I forgot how.

Ghazal

it is dark here & still you have al nur at your neck when fajr does not come
my body is the color of mourning / not dua or dawah / so I say let the day come

my body is fajr / day is mourning / I am still a clot of blood looking for skin
the color of god is a stain / shaped to you like a grief not yet come

black is the color of god not grief & rain is not looking for skin / but is red dust
stepping into your body without melting & finding every empty space a dwelling
to come

I am still an accident of geography looking for a body that is not a stain & prayer
is the mourning I wake up to / the clot of blood I pick until again a wound comes

out the color of accident / which is red dust / the color of geography / which is
dissolution
& lined like a palm made by prayer / shaped to me like a drought not yet come

& yes / I want to be named to the marrow / make inventory & god of what has
yet hurt me
& so I pick dua from your neck until I am no longer wound & strained & come

to claim the dwelling of you a sign & beget a desert of new names & call fajr skin
that has left blood & black how I step into your body & melting the stain to come

it is mourning here / I am four droughts old again & mistake all the women
in my family to the time of desert / clot of blood & red clay straining / for a
homecoming

but looking for skin does not unstitch the mouth & the stain of grief is finding
no words at all & every empty space is like stepping into red dust & what comes

from accident begets home / invented by all the god in my color & yes / I want
to be shaped to the clot / whole & make blood & black of what has yet come

What Use Is Knowing Anything If No One Is Around

What use is knowing anything if no one is around
to watch you know it? Plants reinvent sugar daily
and hardly anyone applauds. Once as a boy I sat
in a corner covering my ears, singing Qur'anic verse

after Qur'anic verse. Each syllable was perfect, but only
the lonely rumble in my head gave praise. This is why
we put mirrors in birdcages, why we turn on lamps

to double our shadows. I love my body more
than other bodies. When I sleep next to a man, he becomes
an extension of my own brilliance. Or rather, he becomes
an echo of my own anticlimax. I was delivered

from dying like a gift card sent in lieu of a pound
of flesh. My escape was mundane, voidable. Now
I feed faith to faith, suffer human noise, complain
about this or that heartache. The spirit lives in between

the parts of a name. It is vulnerable only to silence
and forgetting. I am vulnerable to hammers, fire,
and any number of poisons. The dream, then: to erupt
into a sturdier form, like a wild lotus bursting into

its tantrum of blades. There has always been a swarm
of hungry ghosts orbiting my body—even now,
I can feel them plotting in their luminous diamonds

of fog, each eying a rib or a thighbone. They are
arranging their plans like worms preparing
to rise through the soil. They are ready to die
with their kind, dry and stiff above the wet earth.

A Boy Steps into the Water

and of course he's beautiful
goosebumps over his ribs
like tiny fists under a thin sheet   the sheet
all mudwet and taste of walnut

and of course I'm afraid of him
of the way keeping him a secret will make him
inevitable   I will do anything to avoid
getting carried away   sleep nightly with coins

over my eyes   set fire to an entire
zodiac   mecca is a moth
chewing holes in a shirt I left
at a lover's house   a body loudly

consumes days and awaits the slow
fibrillation of its heart   a lightning rod
sits in silence until finally   the storm
now the boy is scooping up minnows

and swallowing them like a heron
I'm done trying to make sense
of any of this   no one will believe anything
that comes out a mouth like mine

Ordinary Scripture

Everything haunts: sex, hands. If your house wants rain, so be it.
Against the white sheets our bodies are dark treble clefs,

our skin making a sound like ant wings or ghosts. We love
because it makes a mockery of our fathers, the roaming clock

bystander to our teeth against teeth. I burrow across the sheets
like a shark. I spend my mornings circling the bars,

watching videos of radium, green and cool as a lovemark.
I miss the periodic table, all those shy, telepathic letters.

There was a chemistry teacher years ago, who held my hand
while I cried. I used the word *queer*. I haven't since.

It's summer now. When the wind stirs the honeylocusts,
an olive snow falls. We shine flashlights,

walk in the almost-dark until we reach the docks. Wet grass.
A fish hook, tangled in our bikinis and empty coolers.

In the end, we remake love over and over, like unwed atoms,
into forgery, into need, busying our hands with forks, unmade beds,

the magnolia trees, whatever quiet is the one we can bear.

Any Other Name

Khadijah means wife of the prophet.
Nothing about my name
is casual. Your mouth has to
make an effort. You have to commit
to all eight letters, all three syllables,
no nickname. It means something

Uber drivers, the Muslim ones,
all men, want to tell me about
even after I say yes when they ask
do I know. They want to know
how old I am and where I'm from
they want to get in my business

where is my husband. Some men
can't stop telling me who I am or what
exactly is so incredible about me or
what they had to take or offer
without asking. They still say

it's my fault I am beautiful. I was raised
as a Muslim. In the name of Allah
Most Gracious Most Merciful shouldn't I
thank God for the kind of beauty
that makes me so desirable an object

so in demand by strangers
you might say my name cursed me
to solitude. I don't see any prophets around,
do you? If so, pass out my number
tell him I said what's up

where have you been all my life. I know it's a line
but people like familiar things
like fellow boring straight people hey

I'll be 44 in a few years and I have a tradition
to live up to a prophecy perhaps. Chop chop.

I cut off my hair because I wanted to
begin again with something on my body
no man has touched. I wanted to press
rewind. I still want the kind of purity that cures
men of acculturated entitlement. I want a little
silence when I walk down the street or get into the back
seat of a hired car in any city I travel to. Maybe

I have to marry myself. Maybe I am my own prophet.
I want to stop reacting and keep creating
and to do that maybe I need a new kind of hijab
that makes me safer unseen, free of both

sound and adornment. I could use that
kind of safety. Sartre said hell is
other people and *by the token of time through the ages,*
surely a French philosopher knows
whether man equals less than desire and *surely*

man is in loss, except those who do good
works, and enjoin one another to the truth, and enjoin
one another to patience and constancy. My mother told me
I should keep some things to myself.
She should have said keep yourself to yourself

but it was in her nature to be generous.
I learned that kind of giving
leads to further taking and it's a light that attracts
parasites. What's an ex-Muslim girl to do

keep praying. The world of prophets is elite.
They don't just let anyone in, lol not wives
and sometimes I want to cut myself out
of all possible institutional pictures. Sometimes I am in
a collage I made myself and I have
a new name. I have a name
I have given myself and I'm the only one who knows
what it means. But that doesn't make sense

Bismillah ar-rahman ar-rahim
like the first time I was taken from myself
my father asked me what I learned
and that is what I learned. I learned I had no father
but I could walk in the rain and let my hair rise up
in the night become a black halo *aaameeeeeeeeeeen*
curling closer to my head as if to love it, softly

greeting as if saying peace be unto me. A man
can break you with your own love if you don't
remember who you are among the nonbelievers.
All praises due to the part of me that listens to herself
first. The first time I drew a rose I couldn't stop

layering in new petals. My small right hand
filled the flimsy newsprint with red Crayola
spirals, the lines unbroken, the endless making
as sweet as being out of the order
other people like to think you are born to.

Polymath

If one man can take four wives
And the testimony of two women is equal to one man

Then by that algebra
I will have two lovers

One woman and one man
Or two women and no man

If haraam means forbidden
And haram means sacred space
Then harem is an inbetween place

Unholy and holy
Temple where I frolic with my two wives

Nikia Chaney

morning

I still name things. I still search
for kin for kindness on my elbow
my ashy knees. I still wait for
morning, the shower
promises to clean the sun to burn the bed.
I still chew and swallow feel each spoonful
go down as if I were not there.
I still see captivity, aching through me
His body heavy, my mind pure white
ink dripping down inside. Somewhere in the spine, or the marrow
semen congeals fat on the blade.

Somewhere in California

there is a man.
and inside of him
a home.
with a room made of
dark wooden floors
and chipped white paint on the walls.
sleeping bags, coconut oil,
the wish for a father to come back.
breathe, boy.
Here is a list, heavy
with the names of all
the people that love you
and some groceries you
didn't have to buy
yourself.
Here is a mountain view with
a skyline not too far from it.
Here is the referee's hand
lifting your wrist
at the end of
a boxing match.

Aubade with Sage and Lemon

First I said, yes, here
by the light. The dark
has its own blindfold,
the pearls of the eyes
of anyone who will leave
you—sprig of sage

for your hair, he said.
Rind of lemon for
your fingers, and la
ilaha illallah I whistled,
though the dawn eats
its own faith, rubs aromatics

into the question of what
comes after the next air raid
or bombing or shooting
and the morning is blank
and the sun shines down
on another blatant river

of limbs. First I said,
tomorrow, then, now,
I'll leave now, while
it's still safe. A few
more minutes, love,
he said, a few more

hours. Just trust,
he said. I said yes
to the sprig of sage
and the rind of lemon
until the uniformed man
smiled and raised his gun

higher towards the sound
a human body makes
when it's about to fly.
I made no sound
but the sound a wraith
makes as it starves

itself goodbye.
I said sprig, said rind—
and watched him die.
First I begged, grave.
Then I said, above, and lifted
the pen in my wing even higher.

100 Bells

My sister died. He raped me. They beat me. I fell
to the floor. I didn't. I knew children,
their smallness. Her corpse. My fingernails.
The softness of my belly, how it could
double over. It was puckered, like children,
ugly when they cry. My sister died
and was revived. Her brain burst
into blood. Father was driving. He fell
asleep. They beat me. I didn't flinch. I did.
It was the only dance I knew.
It was the kathak. My ankles sang
with 100 bells. The stranger
raped me on the fitted sheet.
I didn't scream. I did not know
better. I knew better. I did not
live. My father said, I will go to jail
tonight because I will kill you. I said,
She died. It was the kathakali. Only men
were allowed to dance it. I threw
a chair at my mother. I ran from her.
The kitchen. The flyswatter was
a whip. The flyswatter was a flyswatter.
I was thrown into a fire ant bed. I wanted to be
a man. It was summer in Texas and dry.
I burned. It was a snake dance.
He said, *Now I've seen a Muslim girl*
naked. I held him to my chest. I held her
because I didn't know it would be
the last time. I threw no
punches. I threw a glass box into a wall.
Somebody is always singing. Songs
were not allowed. Mother said,
Dance and the bells will sing with you.
I slithered. Glass beneath my feet. I
locked the door. I did not
die. I shaved my head. Until the horns

I knew were there were visible.
Until the doorknob went silent.

H.H.

QM

I.
On June 12, 2016
A gunman used religion to justify massacring people who were gathered to celebrate
Their bodies folded into origami
floating towards the heavens as paper cranes
The teal, mustard, and cotton candy hues morphed into dank coffins
This was the deadliest mass shooting in modern America
Yellow and brown skinned rainbows laid bloody
This tragedy occurred during Ramadan, our holy month
This tragedy occurred during Pride, our holy month
To the people who deny the existence of queer Muslims
We are standing here
When one of my identities is killed in the name of another
I become both victim and perpetrator
both sorry and waiting for apology
both gunshot and bullet wound

II.
I too am America
I too am digging my lineage through the debris
I too am a subject of hate based catastrophe
I too am exercising the freedom of religious conviction
I too am trying to wring the guilt out of my skin and release it into freshwater
I too am trying to trace over erasure marks to find myself
I too am still reminding the world of the crossroads in my identity

III.
In queer spaces
I'm only ever seen as an ally
In Muslim spaces
I'm only ever seen as straight.
both sides refuse to love me at the same time
Existing authentically is my jihad
Islam is not a monolith
I am sorry and angry

I am Muslim and queer
I refuse to silence this part of me any longer
Do not tell me I cannot worship God while loving who I want
I will not let my sexuality be invisible so my religion can exist

IV.
But Islam does not equal intolerance
Islam equals acceptance
Visibility does not come from silence
Muslims and non-Muslims deny my existence
Queers and non-queers deny my existence
Conservatives and liberals deny my existence
The imperialist-white-supremacist-capitalist patriarchy denies my existence
This is the first step to acceptance
You cannot erase something without acknowledging it was there to begin with.
My intersections are a double wasp sting
lodged between heart and physique

V.
I too am Muslim
I too am Queer
I too am other
And I will not stop being *Other*
I will not stop standing for justice
Give us a chance to affirm our identities
Stop defining a person's devotion by who they love
We
Are on the cusp of liberation
We
will cascade down the river-bend arm in arm
Heads covered and uncovered
Palms folded and unfolded
Singing of how we had been free all along
Come liberation
We will still be standing here
Waiting to uplift those like us
Who have fallen before

Lily Jamaludin

For Xulhaz

I.
every time the machete
came down
they slashed a knife
down their own
abdomens everything
unraveling fresh
crimson
ribbon   later that night
they pray
fists clenched
to a god they
murdered inside themselves

II.
Xulhaz
I cannot stop looking
at the photo of you
with your eyes closed

face pointed towards
heaven.

somebody else's
hands cupped around
your ears.

Your expression,
something
like a serenity
or peace

though those aren't
the words I'm looking
for

Your body
was once
someone's altar

Is
still someone's son

III.
my stomach coils
I am mourning
for the boys
who are not able
to be boys
for the lovers
trying to walk
each other home

that morning you
thumbed
a book of poems and
felt the sun on your arms
Maybe said a prayer
maybe it went
something like this:

IV.
dear god
i am trying
to understand
why we must
fight so hard
to love
so softly

V.
they used the word

hacked.

VI.
in the photo,   your face.

the word I am looking for
is
sacred.

Blush

if i am the one to sing her into a new body
let it be a sweet rebirth
a ripe pear slipping out of its weathered skin

let it be her mouth

if i am to answer to anything
let it be her mouth
or the pink of it
its freak and spit and loyal tongue

if i am to answer to anything
let it be her cheek
or the flurry of heat rising beneath it
i am blush and the men agree
too often
the men have forgotten their tongues

at home
if i am to answer to anything
let it be the wine and its furnace
let it be the soft cyclone of burning sage
let it be her name
a thousand times
coated
in mango and chili
in ash
in blood
as long as the taste lingers
as long as it slows the hollowing

if i am to answer to anything
let it be the moon
the naked brown witch
the Holy cry of ecstasy
let it be punk

or
at least it's leathered aesthetic
at least then, something Black and skinned will live
at least here, fire is alive
at least if we are burning
we are
doing something

On Longing

An exaggeration that exaggerates. A smile that eats the mouth. Sediment or
beloved, the hanged terrarium.
Want never comes without atonement. Even the fates must share
an eye and a tooth while stroking Apollo's thread. Ask the Sufis how
to find God: buried.
Beneath the ink breath of otherwise; moaning
is is is in circumference. Faith was easier before sex became involved.
Who will touch me in the middle of this war.

Hazem Fahmy

Clubbing w/ Hamed Sinno

And across the dance floor,
a man looks at me
smiling a sun into the room,
hushing the beat like a martyr.
But there is no death here,
only eulogy
for the body,
and how quickly it forgets
the unfathomable.
I hold his hand,
and we sway,
maybe to the music,
maybe to our breaths.
Who knows.
Who cares.
A violin wails
out of excitement
for once.
And he takes me
by the waist,
tells me not be afraid
of the neon, flailing
all around us.

In Which Iblis Lies Awake at Night

I've been waiting
for the moon
to come around and give
me a kiss. Instead,
he just looks
back, blankly, reaching
through the sky, hands
pale and cold. The breeze
stops by, an unwelcome
guest, but I take
what I can get. The balcony
shakes with my body,
a gentle rattle
of old bones
waiting for a resting
place. I touch my skin
and it shivers, afraid
of what might happen
if it's split open,
a ship sinking in
its own blood. Bodice
broken on the floor,
stockings ripped
in the corner. My lipstick
smudged on the cup
I clasp, nail polish chipped
and grotesque. The earth
calls me: habibi,
she says, I saw your face
in the river, floating down
stream, as if escaping
from some kind of burning.
I waited,
but the rain never came.

June 6th

say in that week of june the pipes
did not run dry, and the heat was wet,
and the humidity made the ceiling drip and swell
and i could recite the prayer for rain— if you pray
with a mouth of grief then only lightning will come,
and the warmth of the air
turned you into a damp spot on my neck,
rather than a dark shadow at my rib,
would it be the wet season
again, the time i turn into flood, the swell of your breath,
and wear the dresses you like to touch
me in until i am a faint blur of yellow and cotton, collecting
rain water in metal jugs and dreaming
of roofs not made of tin that sound
like tin when the storms come, or would i simply slip
into your body like a song heard in the womb,
shake your spine into water and drink
until we are somewhere among god's seven skies?

Forbidden

for and *after* Shirin Neshat

When you sang your body invented us
an alphabet. No one heard it
but me.

The earth in your eyes
is the ink in your words.
Each look writes another line.

Everything I need to know grows wings
and lands on my skin.
A thousand tiny plovers

cover the skies, and shine
like moonlight on us both,
turning us into your verses.

Last night each dot and curve of the letters of our alphabet
came to rest on my body while I slept,
entwined around my hips,

pulled their fingers through my hair.
I breathed them in. Became the song
you sang me.

You spell the morning prayer
uttered by my lips.
Syntax of attention

at the back of your throat. Each rise in note
is your hand on my ribs.
You hold me and no one can see.

Our unholy wholeness hides.
Your name in the nearness. Says listen.
Sentences of rebellion

in the starless night.

There needs to be a different word

I don't know why the song is on repeat. If we'd given it another shot the apartment would have exploded. We could've been sued. In the brink of it I felt like spending every day watching grass curl, just by looking at it. By January I needed a new body. Our faucet is still leaking.

I'm not getting what I want so you're a bad person. I didn't prefer a date but thought you'd think I was a slut if I offered to hang in my room again, even though I just wanted to smoke and talk and listen to the new Black Moth.

Both of our parents are brown so we'll get along, right? It's a question of how to enjoy trash media and still be a good person. Teach me how to be gay. I will never go clubbing again, ever.

Faggot is a generous word because I can use it to reclaim myself or be rude depending on my needs. My mom wished I would keep getting diplomas, it didn't matter what kind. She's trying to set me up with her neighbor's daughter. I only want to be friends, really. I want to help her choose a hairstyle and give dating advice. My mom doesn't know we've already agreed to fake-date.

You post a hot pic and it makes me jealous so I post one too and now it looks like we're planning a threesome because we're monogamous after all, and it's not that we fear the other leaving for those liking our posts the day after a fight, even though we said we were good and had sex after.

The first time I heard a bomb it was actually the sound barrier breaking. It was louder than a bomb. If I say it one more time I become a target.

It takes more energy to hate than to ignore. I can still learn how to draw and decide no, but also I don't hate you and it's ok that you moved to LA. I would have been down but I grew up there is all.

I know what you want me to say, but I'm just saying there are plutocrats in brown countries complaining about white people. Rich brown people who won't admit the context makes them analogous to the white people they drag on bad days. Maybe they do know.

Pretending not to be in love is turning out to be hard. I preempted this by saying I was busy and wanted nothing serious. I preempted feeling anything on the ride home when I tripped and pretended not to check if you saw.

Can't tell if I want to adopt a cat because I love cats or I'm just sad. Can't tell if I'm sad or if we ran out of milk when I craved cereal.

I exclusively fall for the sons of immigrant mothers they at some point fell in love with. Mine taught me love and attachment were kind of the same. Now when she calls its always "What did you eat?" and "How is your health?" Sometimes twice in a day.

Institutions are bad but one of them gave us a room to basically trash for a month. I didn't come over because it was late and I had work the next morning. I want to be in love but not publicly, if that makes sense?

What's the word for empathizing with your mom so much that you start to cry at the same things? I should learn how to end something. Please stop me from being wistful. If you play No Doubt, we'll never leave.

There is something about distance that makes Fontana feel like a neon fantasyland. It is a holiday at an immigrant church and not the second generation's fault they perform nostalgia. Christians from Beirut say they are French because of archways in the mall they built there. I am interested in Sufism as a stoner alternative.

I get to your room with the wrong snacks but it's cool because I have the next Kardashians episode and we are past pretending our watching it is anthropological. Is anyone else coming? I believe it when you say it's not that serious. After, you scroll through Tumblr porn while I call home on your fire escape.

There needs to be another way of saying no to hanging or "I don't smoke." You said it would have been better if I actually wanted to help. I told you about when having ideals felt more like narcissism than helping people, which actually involves giving something up.

V.

ZAKAT

Eid in Red and White

+

A heady poppy in the Northwest Frontier of Pakistan, I am a girl in a white frock, ruffled and crumpled all over, red silk ribbons dangling around from the lace collar of it, the puffed sleeves. The fibers in the stiff lattice pattern of a flowery iron fence clench the circumference of my upper arms, synthetic silk pretty and asphyxiating around a torso too young for such tightness, still made only of skin and ribs.

What little air rests in my little lungs seeps out in one punch like popping a balloon when I look up from the preoccupation of youthful unknowing, look up from collecting flowers in a fist, look up from humming songs about bumblebees and twirling until the world blurs, look up and the scene steadies itself as I see it—a lamb all white and wounded, dangling headless from a tree and gushing red blood in steady silken streams that collect into a hot pool. The crimson cruelty of what the supple earth refuses to absorb grabs at my feet in worthless desperation, and I am startled but not at once sickened.

I want to cry, but I don't. I want to run, but I don't. A small drop of red blood falls from the white lamb and lands on the red ribbon of my white dress—remains there, too small and scared to scream murder.

+

"I saw an animal slaughtered only once, I was little and in Pakistan. I think it was a lamb, but it might have been a goat, I can't really remember now." I wish there were something more to say, but can't come up with anything.

I think of the tree the animal was lassoed from, the one from which the jamaan fall, the little purple plum things that pucker up your mouth when you eat them. The tree fills with parrots in the day and bats in the night—they circle it like vultures, in turn. I want to tell him about this, about how the jamaan fall and stain the ground a deep violet—the color of passion as it rises up in the chest, but I don't think he knows what jamaan are. I don't know if there's even a word for them in English. I can't be certain that they exist anywhere but in that strip of land outside my grandfather's house, in my memory of that garden bordered with rose bushes, trimmed with brick along an iron gate that reaches up in spirals, teal and gold, oiled at the hinges and always cool to the guard's rough palms—this much I know.

"Did you think it was disgusting? Did you stop eating meat?" And then I am reminded of just how strange such slaughter is to someone who knows nothing of Eid or the hunger that precedes it. Those who share my memories of the holiday know nothing of him, although I've mentioned to them the things he's told me, described the places we've been together, editing his presence out of the recounting so he's not even a shadow beneath my feet. He has kneaded my skin out of the mould I was poured into, and no one has ever thought to look for his fingerprints on my flesh or maybe he has hidden them well enough, a master sculpture or criminal mastermind. If my parents find out, they might kill me, I think—and it's not just an expression. If they actually knew me, they might hate me. Can something that is not known be loved?

I am tempted to tell him how vile the very idea of consuming flesh became to me, because saying anything else seems cold-blooded. Repulsion before an actual slaughter seems the only rational reaction now in times of processing and packaging away our barbarity, but I can't tell him I found the sacrifice sickening or sacred or anything at all.

The blood was burning red, glowing red, but not anything to make the skin crawl. I didn't find it grotesque, I wasn't alarmed but intrigued, blame this on naivety, for I was too young to even remember how old I was then and although I loved animals, I didn't mind the death of them. I collected insect carcasses in ziplock bags, had a rabbit's foot keychain in hot pink that I lost one day and still miss. My brother and I collected up birds in our hands, wounded broken-winged babies that'd fallen from beneath nurturing mothers, or else flown into garage windows seeing through them but not into them, cutting their bellies on the glass. Somehow, the insides of animals and their many disconnected parts weren't frightening to me, and more clearly than the animal's execution, I remember playing with its entrails.

I tell him about finding them in a heap back by the gate. Tell him, "Someone yelled at us, but I wanted to tear that smooth gray sheet, the intestinal wall I guess, the stomach or something. I dropped this brick on it, but that wasn't enough to cut it, so I pressed down on the brick with my foot until all this shit squished out." I imagine this, a small white-sandaled foot, brick, shit—such is the curiosity of a child, pouring out from the prim package it's dressed in like all the guilt I have kept tucked away inside myself, unseen but always churning. If slaughter becomes sacrifice by the invocation of God's name, the mention of his mercy, I wonder what else can be turned inside out—if a forbidden love can ever be sanctified, made sacred even if His magnanimity is not pronounced, a marriage never proclaimed.

+

I never saw another animal hung after that. In our Northwest Ohio home, it came to us cut, cubed, cleaned as if these animals were never anything but their flesh. This was always troublesome to my parents. They had a bloodthirst that went unquenched by merely calling in orders at halal butcher shops, picking up bags, marked and sealed, of sacrificial lambs. Over long-distance phone calls to even distant relatives, they asked of the size, weight, type of livestock slaughtered, demanding details—where the animal was hung from, who slit its throat, if it bucked and brayed so as to make real the images in their mind, and, with the blood of those distant beasts, commemorate Eid with a holy water that courses deep red.

Why Activist Blair Imani Will No Longer Wear Hijab Post-Trump

As I watched Hillary Clinton's chances of winning the presidency dwindle last Tuesday night, I remembered that this presidential campaign has awakened and empowered a side of America that has always been here. In Times Square, looking at the giant LED screen that showed an increasing number of states turning red, I thought about my commute from Bushwick into Manhattan that morning. While being visibly Muslim on any form of transportation is a less than comfortable experience, I felt like I was under a more menacing magnifying glass than usual. I felt like my presence was more noticed and further unwanted. Donald Trump's rhetoric of bigotry, discrimination, and scapegoating has been felt by all oppressed people. Unfortunately, it has also given people with hate in their hearts a license to act on their biases.

I saw four white male Trump supporters in their red hats walk past me in Times Square, and I felt their gaze in a new way. I looked at them wondering how they could live among people like me and disregard the consequences presented by a Trump presidency. I wondered if they saw me as human. And Donald Trump is not unique in his bigotry. I have felt a hostile gaze at Hillary Clinton rallies as well. Once, a fellow Hillary supporter called me a terrorist.

Taking all of this into account, I tweeted: "I'm scared that today will be the last day I felt somewhat safe wearing my hijab." I said "somewhat safe" because bigotry didn't manifest overnight or even because of Donald Trump. Bigotry is as American as I am. Still, the majority of my fellow Americans refuse to recognize this.

I wore my traditional hijab for a few hours on the morning of Wednesday, November 9. (I converted to Islam in college, in May 2015, and began wearing hijab full time in March 2016.) I sent a note into work letting folks know I would be offline the whole day. People at work were supportive and understanding; this was not the case for everyone I encountered. As I ran some errands I felt an even more intense gaze than the day before, I was even stopped on the train. A woman came up to me on the verge of tears, mouthing the words, "I'm sorry." While it was obvious that she meant well, it was also very apparent that something had changed. And I did not feel safe.

My decision to take a break from wearing hijab was made when I got a call from journalist, filmmaker, and activist Rokhaya Diallo indicating that she wanted to interview me near Trump Tower. Trump Tower felt like the epicenter of Trump's America and I was certain that his supporters would be even more empowered by the sheer proximity to their leader. I did not think twice before walking to the nearest clothing store to buy a hat.

I changed clothes and lamented what felt to me like a step toward safety. I mourned the death of American freedom, as bigotry and the very real threat of physical violence scared me from exercising the right to express my faith.

While hate crimes continue to be reported, well-meaning allies have urged me to continue wearing hijab, to protest, to be "brave." I thought to myself, What shame is there in hats? What shame is there in protecting myself? I know my fear is valid, but it seemed like folks were eager to doubt me. I am unapologetically Black and I am unapologetically Muslim. My faith is not dependent on my adherence to a given individual's perception of Islam. Moving forward I will stay covered, whether that means wearing hats, beanies, or berets. It is not cowardice that is informing my decision, it is survival.

As a Black American Muslim woman I am fully aware of the reality of discrimination in this country. Like many Americans, my lived experience is not a simple one; I live at the intersection of Islamophobia, anti-Blackness, and misogyny. Trading my hijab for more "palatable" head coverings does not liberate me from bigotry, it makes me feel a bit more safe.

The glimmer of hope that I hold on to now is that Trump's administration will unite marginalized people toward a common goal and force allies to realize that they must center the voices and lived experiences of marginalized people. If all of us who comprise "the other" are given the space and liberty to enact the path toward our collective liberation, I believe it will come a lot sooner. For folks of privilege, this means having uncomfortable conversations at the dinner table, speaking up against hate, and taking steps to be a genuine ally.

The next four years will undoubtedly be a period of huge challenges for marginalized people, so I urge everyone to exercise self-care and remember: bravery comes in many forms.

Editor's Note: After Trump's election, Blair Imani stopped wearing the hijab only temporarily.

Fariha Róisín

How I Learned to Accept My Queerness as a Muslim Woman

+

Language is important. It gives voice to ideas, but most importantly: to feelings. When I was a young teen I didn't understand why I felt attracted to all sexes, not just to the opposite of mine. I went to an all-girls school and I felt the blossoming of bodies near me with such intrigue. I had politically radical parents, but not when it came to sex. Sex was an unformed, vacuous thing that nobody wanted to unpack. Like an elephant in the room, it felt like a bone stuck in my throat. I wanted to know what sex was like. I wanted to know what sex was like with everybody. Coming from a Muslim family, I never felt pressure to be anything, but I did feel a pressure to be desexualized. I felt my desire like a blush that went up my body. I didn't know why I felt attracted by everyone, that everything could turn me on. Then things changed.

I remember reading this article when I was fourteen, fifteen—in those stages of my mid-teens and early, early pre-adulthood, where ideas have a relevance towards your fast-shifting self-perception. Where the information acquired from different oscillating inspirations is vital to your construct of personhood. So much so that they become beacons of how you see yourself, they become parts of your moulded identity. They calcify who you are like flesh and bone.

The said article was in the Books section of the *Sydney Morning Herald,* an Australian national newspaper my father never read. But one day, accidentally, we started receiving it on the daily, and I felt delusional and subversive about getting a somewhat watered-down liberal-ish newspaper for free—it was like we were beating the system. On this day, the page in question was lying face up when I saw it folded over the hip of our moss green sofa; its edges beckoned me. The drawing on the cover was of two men, and I recognized it to be in the traditional style of Mughal art. They were holding each other, in a somewhat candid, familiar embrace, like two nightingales, curved towards each other, brooding lips, full, mellifluous, eyes, and bushy eyebrows. They looked just like me. I was transfixed and seduced and moved. When you're young you crave anything that might be an explanation for who you are, and you seek it out like a dark treat. I consumed the piece.

 The article was about queerness in Islam. Particularly amidst its rulers, such as Abu Nuwas, a ruler of modern-day Iran; Al-Amin, the sixth Abbasid Caliph, Mahmud of Ghazni, the ruler of the Ghaznavid Empire; and even the famous Mehmed the Conqueror (the famous Ottoman sultan of the fifteenth century). These men, historically, were all known to have favored men, meaning that these men were gay—in modern terms.

+

Poetry and art about love between two men were seen in the Muslim world as natural, or even normal. Even the poems by perhaps Islam's most famous poet, Rumi, talk about his love for his best friend, Shams of Tabriz. The love between them is almost hagiographic. It's seminal.

The *Encyclopedia of Islam and the Muslim World* says:

> Whatever the legal strictures on sexual activity, the positive expression of male homoerotic sentiment in literature was accepted, and assiduously cultivated, from the late eighth century until modern times. First in Arabic, but later also in Persian, Turkish and Urdu, love poetry by men about boys more than competed with that about women, it overwhelmed it. Anecdotal literature reinforces this impression of general societal acceptance of the public celebration of male-male love (which hostile Western caricatures of Islamic societies in medieval and early modern times simply exaggerate).

As I read this my tortured viscera of longing to be understood subsided, and for a few wonderful seconds I realized I wasn't an anomaly. Feelings of evil are commonly projected onto anything that's not understood, and though I had never felt the intense persecution of my sexuality, I had always felt it lingering. I always felt my cheeks deepen darker when women would gaze at me, and though I was obsessed with boys, my thoughts of women were so much more intense, like a bruise that felt both painful and pleasurable to the touch.

+

I don't think I ever realized I was gay, or bisexual, or queer—or any of these things. I always just felt like me, a teen—maybe a particularly horny one.

I went to an all-girls school with a pink uniform, and I had crushes on everyone. One girl named Cynthia who was a couple of grades older than me looked like Chris Martin when I liked Chris Martin. I was thirteen, and Coldplay hadn't started making shitty rock-pop songs yet. I called her up once to invite her to an event I was hosting and had organized in conjunction with my school's social justice club (which I was the president of) for a Tsunami Relief effort. In late December of 2004, a tsunami devastated several coasts lined along the Indian Ocean. The tsunami killed 230,000 people in fourteen countries—Indonesia was the hardest hit, but there were also large death tolls in Thailand, Sri Lanka, and Somalia. My school raised $25,000. I was on TV for a few seconds, and there was even a newspaper article about our efforts. My cohort and I celebrated our activism—we were the brave girls who cared so much about the world, and we were impressed by our power. We were told we were the future leaders. Afterwards, I wanted to call Cynthia up and say "We did it!" I don't think we ever talked again.

Then, I liked my history teachers. Miss O, my ancient history teacher—(unmarried); my modern history teacher; Mrs. C—(married and, at one point, pregnant); a girl named Lauren who was, like, a smooth five years older than me. She basically graduated high school the year I started and had spiky black hair and big eyes that narrowed on me every time I'd walk past her, staring with frightened cajoling smiles. Then I fell deeply in love with my best friend, whose name is *Color* in Japanese. She was perfect—and then that was that.

+

See, while I explored my sexuality and simultaneously worked part time for Oxfam and Amnesty wanting to save the world, I was also a normal Muslim kid. I fasted, I learned the surahs, I read the Qur'an, I learned Arabic, and had an utmost surging belief in God (I still do). My intrigue in the workings of my sexuality didn't feel like the antithesis of what I was learning, or feeling, or understanding about being Muslim, or even Islam. In fact, I felt my love for God, for Islam, for the Prophet, as a companion for my love for the exploration of myself—and of the world around me. I didn't think they were things that were mutually exclusive. I just knew that people wouldn't understand, and that kids, who always have an inherent understanding of pathos, would.

I was never open about my sexuality with anyone around me, whether they were my secular, non-Muslim friends or my Muslim ones. I never knew how to be open about something that felt so liminal and dynamic. I knew I liked men, but I also liked women. How was that possible? At fourteen, I did tell a white friend "I think I'm bisexual," but being so frank about something so misunderstood felt callous without any further explanation. I had nothing to really say about it, but I did feel like I had to acknowledge that part of me—though, because I was already different (brown, Muslim), I didn't want to add my sexuality to the list. I felt somewhat guarded about it. I understood that there was a taboo, but maybe with all things in my life I've felt that society—that people—would eventually come to see it my way. I was an uncharacteristically hopeful young kid. I somehow knew at some point I'd be able to give voice to these feelings. My friend never asked me about being bisexual again.

+

When Muslimism is policed by governments, by institutions in power (in 2016 the Prime Minister of the United Kingdom, David Cameron, described Muslim women as being "traditionally submissive"), it disillusions the public and its rational engagement with Islam, and it confuses Muslims (young and old) into thinking that there is some truth in false statements. So, they then either dispute Islam in an attempt to side with "modernity" (the typical response of younger Muslims) or they embrace these points, believing that if God says women are inferior, then the statements must be right (the typical response of older Muslims). Neither of those two sides decides to do any research on its own. Instead, they blithely decide to believe what other people tell them. Ignorance is bliss.

The comments Mr. Cameron made are intensely bigoted: propagating a myth that Muslims are intolerant to progressiveness is upsetting. Too often metaphors are used against Islam to tarnish it as a backward religion, and to imply that Islam has neither nuance nor relevancy, and therefore it has no validity in the modern world. For the over 1.5 billion people who self-identify with Islam, well, we are seen as unknowingly misguided. Muslims are treated as the cipher for the world's problems.

If we can't engage openly with our faith because it's been demonized culturally, how can we be expected to navigate our identities in the complex ways in which we should? If people are told that they are wrong, then how are they able to sincerely like themselves and accept everything they are? For so long, because of my own shame, I diluted my existence. It was too terrifying to be all the things that I am, so I picked and chose parts of myself, hiding the rest away.

What has happened in the post-9/11 world to Muslims has done more damage to the Muslim psyche than any other thing. The feelings of rage I had for myself are tethered to the feeling of being unwanted. Every person of color has felt this to some extent—the fear of being seen as completely wrong, and being so terrified that at any moment someone might disclose to you how ugly, or worthless, you really are. In these circumstances we've whitewashed ourselves in the hope of being accepted. In subliminal (and sometimes blatant) ways we are taught that white is good, white is beautiful, white is better—so we customize ourselves to appease the oppressor. We believe in the oppressor's language so wholeheartedly, and yes, we want to change, we want to be like them. Until we don't. Until we realize that there is a great beauty to our existence, just as we are.

+

I understand that it is my choice to experience Islam in a way I believe emphasizes our humanity. God is the only judge, and as humans our responsibility is to not spew hate, but to love one another in a holistic and profound way. The shadows of Islam's philosophies define my reality. Faith—Islam—has always been my foundation. I am Muslim because I believe in God—and therefore I believe in his mercy, his kindness. I don't believe religion to be puritanical, or dogmatic—that's never been its design. Even as a kid, when deathly sermons were read in front of me about hellfire and fear, it never resonated. God to me has always signified the best of our paltry human goodness. God is better than all of us.

Not too long ago a good Muslim friend of mine wrote to me: "I have a hard time believing in any deity who would create us as flawed, instinctive people, and then punish us for acting in ways that are flawed or instinctual. That seems too cruel. There has to be more love than that. It strikes me as important that in the Qur'an God is most often referred to as All-Merciful. I think about the capacity we, as humans, have for mercy. The number of people we forgive on a daily basis: our parents, for not being who we want them to be, our siblings, our shitty, flaky friends, our forgetful lovers, our terrible neighbors, our own corrupted selves. If *that* is what mere *human* mercy looks like, then a Godlike mercy must have a capacity for so much more."

The smartest thing Nietzsche ever said was "there are no facts, only interpretations."

This is my interpretation of Islam. I believe it to be more powerful to resist hatred, than to sink into it, and succumb. I believe it to be more powerful to love what we don't know, or understand, then to disregard it. That is not our place, that is not our responsibility. I've always thought of faith as a selfless practice. To love others, with no hope of a reward, is nirvana.

+

I've never been a believer in the reformation of Islam, but I have been a believer in the reformation of Muslims. We forget that God's patience and love are what made us, and that true enlightenment is seeking a place of peace, surrendering, and looking inward for change. I hate that sexuality is a moralist conversation instead of a humanist one. That people who are born with certain proclivities are tortured into believing their own impudence. That, in the name of God, society can hate with impunity. When did we get so weak as a species? Have we learnt nothing about humanity through the ages?

For many years I believed in my self-disgust. I shamed myself for my sexuality, believing that's what I had to do. That being me, fully me, was demonic, and I hated myself for it. I was lost, I was terrified, and I was unhappy and in a constant cycle of self-hurt. In retrospect, I wish someone could have said: God made you this way, love yourself. If we teach people to love what they are—naturally they will love others too. When you can learn to heal all that is broken inside of you, when you come to terms with you, and why you're here, you can have a more profound existence. To hate is draining. Keep in mind your own mortality, and the importance of self-forgiveness; the rest will come naturally.

+

I hate to hide anymore because this isn't my purpose in life. My purpose, I feel, is to help others—the other South Asian and Muslim youth—to heal from the trauma from the hate that drives others to tell us, "You're wrong," "You're not good enough," especially when that comes from people that you need to love you the most.

Being queer and accepting that label for myself is about survival. It's about the power we get when words are ascribed to ourselves out of our own choice. When the correct term finds its way to you, it's liberating, like a big sigh of relief. It reminds you that even your strangeness has a function. Being queer and Muslim, and proudly believing in those two identities, is also a way for me to distinguish myself, for myself, against the forces of neoliberal, white-supremacist, imperial-capitalist cis-hetero-patriarchy that so readily want to categorize people into factions. But I will not be contained. I will not be a digestible commodity. If it's challenging for you to understand my distinctions, that says more about you then it says about me.

If people don't understand you, it's probably because they don't need to. They've never had to explore themselves the way you've had to, you shiny, beautiful thing. As Barthes says: "One must pluralize, refine, continuously." Don't be afraid of all that lies within you. Trust in the process of life. Trust in God.

Lamya H

Queer Brown Futures (Or Lack Thereof)

The Idyll

+

For access to which, you have to pretend.

This comes to me jarringly, on a weekend trip home. My parents have just returned from a cousin's wedding in Pakistan, and we're spending a lazy Saturday afternoon splayed out in the living room looking at photos from their trip. *We* as in the extended family, who have strategically draped ourselves around the TV: my uncle, next to the laptop in case of technical difficulties, the cousin, who is a notorious grazer, next to the rapidly depleting *channa chur*, my brother, at an awkward angle on the floor that will allow him to see the screen while being as horizontal as possible.

They're beautiful, the photos. Everyone in their wedding finery, with the colors and the soft lighting designed to play off makeup, hide blemishes, accentuate the bling. We *ooh* and *aah* appropriately. Tell my mother she looks like she's in her thirties, tease my cousin every time an eligible bachelor comes on the screen, giggle at the one person who's always out of sync in the elaborately choreographed dances.

When it strikes me, suddenly—how similar everyone looks. The faces are different, the clothes are different, but there's a certain conformity, an ease of being. If you squint your eyes till shapes blur, everyone seems happy, suitably attired, suitably gendered. All my friends from childhood summers in the motherland, now appropriately coupled and children-ed, with lives proceeding according to plan.

This illusion lasts, of course, only until the gossip starts flowing. Who's being advised to stay in the marriage for the kids; who hasn't been able to hold down a job in years; who is developing a drinking problem.

And yet, we pretend.

 Later that night, me and my older sister volunteer to put the younger ones to bed. Dress them in their pajamas, read them a story, and then, as we lie in the darkened room waiting for them to fall asleep, my older sister begins the lecture that I know is coming. Call the parents more, visit more often, and then, in a quieter voice, tells me that she's worried that I'm beginning to *bhatak*. Deviate.

I breathe in. Wonder if this is code for queerness. Has she heard anything, are there rumors? I ask her to elaborate, in the coolest tone I can muster through my rising panic.

Turns out that it's my short hair. That I cut in spite of my parents' entreaties, that no one sees under my hijab anyway. The fact that I'm living so far away.

I exhale. And wonder how long it'll be possible to pretend.

Freedom

+

For which you have to assimilate. (Into whiteness.)

I realize this, jarringly, on a weekend trip back from a soccer tournament. I'm in a car, navigating while one of my best friends drives, with my teammates sleeping obliviously in the back.

We have known each other for a while, this friend and I. She is one of the first people I talked to about queerness, in abstract terms first and then her queerness and my queerness. She hasn't had an easy time of it: her parents are wealthy, conservative, and expect that her life will play out in certain ways. They have poorly handled her coming out, finding themselves ill prepared for their blond, blue-eyed little girl to grow into a snapback-wearing, hair-shorn short, CrossFit-obsessed lesbian.

And so it comes out of nowhere, her obnoxious comment. We're talking about her parents, how they are finally beginning to come around. How it's the little things—like her mother asking her if she's dating anyone on a recent phone call—that show that they are finally beginning to come around.

"Lamya, you know. You should come out to your family too."

I sigh. I've heard this in so many forms, from so many people that I've stopped engaging.

"I'm serious. It'll be hard at first, but it'll work out in the end. And if it doesn't, if they don't accept you for who you are, they don't deserve your love."

They don't deserve my love. They don't deserve my love, these people who have sacrificed so much for me. These people for whom, in this foreign country where they are markedly different, family is everything, community is everything. They don't deserve my love. I should be me, I should make some loud and proud pronouncement that could cut me off from all that my parents know, all of the futures they think are available to me, and expect them to come around. I should be free.

I'm seething at this point. Grit my teeth to stop anything that I'll regret saying from slipping out. When a voice pipes up from the backseat.

"Hey Lamya, are you even allowed to be gay in your religion?"

We turn to each other, me and my friend, and roll our eyes so hard it is almost audible.

"Ooooh, this is my favorite song," my friend says. "Can you turn it up?"

She doesn't bring it up again.

The Stalemate

+

For which you do, well, nothing. For which you wait it out.

I'm precocious enough at sixteen to realize that any photos in which I'm smiling and dressed in shalwar kameez can potentially be used for arranged marriage set-ups. The kind in which aunties exchange biographical details and photographs and the color of your skin, to set you up with a suitable boy who you talk to for a couple of months before the two of you decide if you're compatible.

I'm not opposed to arranged marriages in principle: my parents had one and I've seen cousins end up in happy situations. A few nasty broken engagements in my family have resulted in a strict no-pressure policy. But it won't work for me, this arranged marriage business, and I can't figure out how to break it to my parents.

That I've been careful with photographs since I was sixteen comes in handy. A decade of steely frowns and uncroppable positioning of friends means that my family has zero rishta pictures, giving me some semblance of control over the process.

My parents try one year, on Eid. I'm dressed up and they ask to take a photograph with me.

"Just one photo where you're smiling, Lamya. Come sit between us."

I tell them I know what they're up to. They concede with nervous giggles.

The next year, they bring it up more directly. I'm in grad school at this point, lucky enough to deploy the one thing they've always emphasized more than anything else: education. This works for a while.

And then, a year ago, I find an innocuous-looking file on our family computer titled "Lamya's profile." I can't help but click it—hoping, praying, fingers and toes crossed, that it's not what I think it is. Of course it is exactly what I think it is: a marriage profile. My education background, hobbies, a concise history of the migration of my family westward. And my passport photo.

I decide not to confront my parents. After all, their efforts don't seem to be working, and maybe silence is more compassionate. This way at least they can feel that they're doing their duty by me.

The next time marriage talk comes up, I claim education again and they surrender again. I figure the subsequent career stages will serve me well in terms of deflection, until I reach some arbitrary age of expiry.

A fragile dance, this. I wonder how sustainable it is, this endless cycle of doing nothing.

Alternatives

\+

Which I know exist. They must.

I've met people living them, in fact. Friends who hide lovers in plain sight as roommates. Queer men and women who cobble together multi-spoke families to make babies, families that double as hetero mirages. Others who have spent years and years and impressive amounts of emotional energy loving, forgiving, and building adult relationships with their parents before bringing up gayness.

Why are these not (also) the stories we tell each other, these stories of alternative futures, these stories of resistance? Why do we only collect coming-out stories, it-gets-better stories, these stories that are set in the past, that tell of a particular set of experiences that not everyone can relate to? Stories that treat the future as if it doesn't come with problems of its own?

Because what are stories for if not this, for finding ourselves in the narratives of others? Reminders that we're not alone, that there are lives available to us outside what we're constantly being told are the only ways to live? Where can we find inspiration and ideas for expanding our imaginations about the radical future except from each other?

So queer brown people, people with no futures, all of you all: this is a call. Let's tell our stories.

Say Ameen

1. this is what i see when i close my eyes to pray.

this is what i see when i close my eyes to sleep.

i am not saying that sleep is prayer. but dreams, those are.

say: ameen.

2. the day after the election we all look at each other differently. for once, *all* meaning: everyone. we notice each other. we *see* each other. eye contact is being made, even welcome. it's as if we're all seeing one another for the first time. we see with an awareness of who we might lose first. that is to say, who is most vulnerable. on the train everyone is solemn, save for two hijabis sitting with a man who is playing videos on his phone that make them laugh. a white woman is watching me watch them with tears in my eyes.

iqra: *i am not interested in the veil that is worn on the head as much as i am in the one between this world and the other. i am not interested in the veil that is worn on the head as much as i am in the one between this world and the other. i am not interested in the veil that is worn on the head as much as i am in the one between this world and the other.*

3. a) i began noticing the veiled women more and more after the elect--n. they have always been part of my world but i seem to see them everywhere now. once when i was apartment hunting i was going to look at a place near a hasidic-jewish neighborhood in bk. i asked my friends to come along. as we approached

the apartment she said, "oh, i'm probably the worst person you could have brought along." i laughed. but it wasn't until a few days later that i realized she meant she was the worst person to bring because she was veiled. b) months later we are trading poems by email for feedback. she worries the ending doesnt land. that "they" wont get it. i tell her the key is to center ourselves. dont worry about they. focus on us. it's like this: if you're holding the camera then just keep it pointed at us, at yourself. zoom in. c) photo description: image inverted. shirin neshat at the whitney banner in the foreground. the american flag waving weakly in the distance. brings bree newsome to mind. i ask: who do you give space to? who do you pay attention to? what is in your gaze? how do you better focus your vision? what tricks will you allow your eyes to play? or your mind?

right, there's nothing there. i stop going because everyone has something to say about everyone else. i stop going because the [children] are rowdy. there is no peace. i stop going because in every mosque they want to tell you how to pray: "raise your finger this way, sister"—wana basabah, "your finger should be steady," i do not ask them why they are more attentive to my prayer than their own. is my sole index finger pointing to mecca, measuring the rhythm of my recitation, that distracting? this is not what the prophet intended. or is there some hassanah for advising your neighbor in prayer i didnt hear about?

i stop fasting in cairo. i stop fasting in cairo when i see the gluttony at iftar. after i gain 40 lbs / 22 kilos on balah il shaam and my sleep cycle is permanently wrecked by the wait for dawn. my auntie is our sheikh at home. she does taraweeh like a sarookh. that is a rocket. her knees crack like my father's. we bring her glucosamine supplements from amreekah.

i remember all the mosques i've attended. here are a few: columbus, ohio: the brown flat carpet with masking tape fading into it to mark the qibla and prayer-row lines. dearborn, michigan: a shi'a mosque where the people put their foreheads to rocks as they prostrate. albuquerque, new mexico: the paki bully sisters. muskegon, michigan: my father goes to meet with brothers who are incarcerated at the local jail here once a week. i go to the mosque where i pray with the same three women every friday. a family of black converts. the mother has knee problems and i notice she cannot fully prostrate. i get her a chair and tell her she can pray seated and show her how. prayer is not meant to be painful. she accepts and i feel guilty knowing she might only trust me because i am an arab and was born into this religion and am, therefore, some kind of authority. never mind what i am here to repent. what i am trying to forget.

Some Kind of Holy

وَلَا تَمْشِ فِي الْأَرْضِ مَرَحًا ۖ إِنَّكَ لَن تَخْرِقَ الْأَرْضَ وَلَن تَبْلُغَ الْجِبَالَ طُولًا

+

On 9/11 I remember my dad, my Muslim dad, my dad with a messy *mullah* beard, my dad who lives in a psychiatric hospital, imprisoned by his fear. My dad who used to take me out for ice cream in the middle of winter, our numb fingers barely able to hold on to our ice cream cones, always the only ones in the shop. My dad who I haven't thought about for weeks, my dad who I try to forget.

The day after Donald Trump is elected president, the day after half the country votes against Muslims, I remember my crazy dad. My brown dad from Pakistan. My dad the rowing champion, my dad the masjid leader. My dad who talks to God in his dreams, my dad an imagined saint. He is *some* kind of holy. My dad who used to drive from city to city, trying to find somewhere he was safe, until he started walking because he thought poison was seeping into his skin from the car seats. My dad whose fear reveals itself in every word he speaks. My dad who scares this country, my dad who scares me, my dad who I try every day not to love.

+

This year, 9/11 is the day before Eid. It is also Arafah, the 9th day of Dhul Hijja, the holiest day in Islam, when Muslims fast to be forgiven for their sins from the year before and the year ahead. I want to be forgiven for loving a Muslim girl, for pretending to be my mother's perfect daughter, for having sex when I wasn't in love, for hating my brown skin, for trying to be white, for getting a B, for not praying enough, for all the times I won't pray in the year ahead.

I fast, too, for my dad. He never missed a fast in his life until Ramadan this year, when he became too sick to fast, when he started believing that fasting was how the government controlled us. I miss my dad who taught me how to pray, who built my faith up so strong it became brittle. My dad who loved my mom. My dad who taught me how to read the Qur'an in Arabic, how to say my God's words, how to say them so softly no one would hear.

+

On the morning of Easter Sunday this year, in one of Lahore's most popular parks, a man standing near the gates lights the fuse on his heavy black vest, starting a chain reaction that ends with an explosive blast, killing seventy-five and injuring hundreds, most of whom are children and their mothers. The earth splits open, never stitches itself back up.

On the morning of Easter Sunday this year, I am at home in Tennessee, where my parents had immigrated almost twenty years ago to provide a better life for my brother and me, much as their parents had traveled to the newly created Pakistan in the mid-twentieth century. My grandparents, though, were not immigrants but refugees, forced to relocate by Hindu nationalists; a kind of Islamophobia I never want to know.

My fear is an American kind, the kind that comes from being the only brown person in my class, from the way my Muslim name gets caught on white tongues. I am a visitor, but I still feel at home in Pakistan; at home in its quiet chaos, in its mountain roads, in the dark mornings when the power goes out and candlelight makes the house feel holy, safe.

+

My cousins, brother, and I spent stretches of our childhood at my grandparents' house in Lahore. Long summer months we would eat mangoes on the roof and converse with the parrots in the shed. One visit was during monsoon season, and the rains started to come. There is no working drainage system in Lahore, so when it rains the whole city sinks in itself, fills to the brim with acidic soup. Citywide, the raindrops tattoo on baked roofs.

Our grandparents' lawn filled with rainwater the color of sewage, unfiltered. We saw it as a swimming pool. My cousins and I had already spent a good twenty minutes swimming outside before our parents discovered us, long enough to contract a combination of viruses and become deathly sick. Now we watch the rain from the windows. The water gets blacker with the years. Sometimes I step outside to taste the drops on my tongue, and they still taste sweet like the summer mangoes my now-blind grandfather cuts for me. His fingers already know all the moves.

+

My mother calls me crying the morning after Donald Trump is elected president. Her grief is an old kind, the kind from her childhood in Pakistan; she was raised to believe that a woman was half of a man. My mother doesn't care that her America makes fun of her accent, tells her to go back to Pakistan, drops bombs in the country she grew up in. My mother's America allowed her to leave her crazy husband, to start from nothing, to work for the first time in her life, to raise her children by willpower alone. Her grief is a new kind, too, wearing the prayer beads on her *tasbeeh* thin, mourning her America that believed in women, even though she knew it didn't believe in her.

Unlike my mother, I have nowhere to go back to. I have always claimed America as my own. Still, white America will always hate me for the brownness of my skin, for the way my name gets caught on their tongues, for the way I remind them of a war they created, of all the Americans killed who were more American than me.

+

The microwave sounds like an arrhythmic heart, the sound of popcorn kernels unfurling in the heat. The smell of smoke seeps out into the room; it will linger in the air for hours to come. It's ten a.m. on my birthday, and I'm sitting alone in my dorm lounge eating burnt popcorn, still slightly drunk from the night before. The popcorn clumps are black, charred blooms. They look like the lotus flowers my mother paints. Dried, crumbling in the palm of my hand. Filling up the corners of the room we share, decaying in a neat line on the floor. There is always paint on the ends of my mother's hair, on the edge of her lips, on her ankles. Nineteen years ago she knit me in her womb. And nineteen years before that she was growing up in an attic room, painting among lizards and dust in the heat.

In Sunday School I learned that heaven is found beneath my mother's feet. When we go on walks, my mother opens herself up to the sky. She creates clouds in our room, hangs fragmented *jalis* from the ceiling, tells me to worship their imperfect geometries. My mother has learned to believe in what she can create. I have learned to believe in her; I worship her warm body next to mine, the sound of her *duas* at night. God, I seek refuge in you, she says over and over again. *Audu'billahi, Audu'billahi, Audu'billahi.* I whisper these prayers along with her in a hundred quiet breaths, praying deep and soft, so soft that I don't know if God can hear.

Practicing Islam in Short Shorts

The scenario I'm about to describe has happened to me more times than I can count, in more cities than I can remember, mostly in Western cities in the U.S. and Europe.

I walk into a store. There's a woman shopping in the store that I can clearly identify as Muslim. In some scenarios she's standing behind the cash register tallying up totals and returning change to customers. She's wearing a headscarf. It's tightly fastened under her face where her head meets her neck. Arms covered to the wrists. Ankles modestly hidden behind loose-fitting pants or a long, flowy dress. She's Muslim. I know it. Everyone around her knows it. I stare at her briefly and think to myself, "She can't tell if I'm staring at her because I think she is a spectacle or because I recognize something we share."

I realize this must make her uncomfortable, so I look away. I want to say something, something that indicates I'm not staring because I'm not familiar with how she chooses to cover herself. Something that indicates that my mother dresses like her. That I grew up in an Arab state touching the Persian Gulf where the majority dresses like her. That I also face East and recite Qur'an when I pray.

"Should I greet her with 'A'salamu alaikum?'" I ask myself. Then I look at what I picked out to wear on this day. A pair of distressed denim short shorts, a button-down Oxford shirt, and sandals. My hair is a big, curly entity on top of my head, still air-drying after my morning shower. Then I remember my two nose rings, one hugging my right nostril, the other snugly hanging around my septum. The rings have become a part of my face. I don't notice them until I have to blow my nose or until I meet someone not accustomed to face piercings.

I decide not to say anything to her. I pretend that we have nothing in common and that I don't understand her native tongue or the language in which she prays. I'm not prepared for a possibly judgmental glance up and down my body. I don't want to read her mind as she hesitantly responds, "Wa'alaikum a'salam."

I'm guilty of judging and projecting my thoughts onto her before giving her a chance to receive this information and respond to it. It's wrong. My hesitation in these scenarios comes from knowing that a sizable number of people from my religion look at people dressed like me and write us off as women who have lost their way and veered off the path of Islam. I don't cover my thighs, let alone my ankles. (The most dominant Islamic schools of thought consider a woman's ankles to be *'awrah*, meaning an intimate part of her body, and revealing it is undoubtedly a sin.) Nothing in my outward appearance speaks to or represents the beliefs I carry. Some might even get to know me and still label me as a non-practicing Muslim—I drink whiskey and I smoke weed regularly.

However, I am a practicing Muslim. I pray (sometimes), fast, recite the travel supplication before I start my car's engine, pay my zakkah (an annual charitable practice that is obligatory for all that can afford it), and, most importantly, I feel very Muslim. There are many like me. We don't believe in a monolithic practice of Islam. We love Islam, and because we love it so much we refuse to reduce it to an inflexible and fossilized way of life. Yet we still don't fit anywhere. We're more comfortable passing for non-Muslims, if it saves us from one or more of the following: unsolicited warnings about the kind of punishment that awaits us in hell, unwelcomed advice from a stranger that starts with "I am like your [insert relative]," or an impromptu lecture, straight out of a Wahhabi textbook I thought was nonsense at age thirteen.

Islamic studies was part of my formal education until I graduated from high school in the United States. The textbooks we used were from Saudi Arabia, which is the biggest follower of the Wahhabi sect of Islam. The first time I realized it was okay to verbalize how nonsensical these books were was when I was watching a movie with my mother about a family that lost one of their children to a terminal disease. I must have been six or seven years old. My mother said something to the effect of, "I know Allah has a special place in heaven for mothers that lose their children at a young age." I looked at my mom and asked her, "Even if they're not Muslim?" Without breaking eye contact with the TV set she responded, "Even if they're not Muslim."

That was all the permission I needed to allow myself to believe in a more compassionate God than the one spoken about in these textbooks. My parents are pretty religious. They don't know I smoke or drink. I'm honestly not quite sure how they would react to knowing that I do, but I'm not exactly ready to find out. They encouraged me and my sister to wear headscarves, but they didn't force us to. Like most parents they didn't want us wearing anything too revealing or attention grabbing. They would not approve of my wearing shorts.

When it became evident that we weren't always praying five times a day, they mostly stayed quiet and occasionally spoke to us about the benefits of prayer.

My mother loved reading novels by American writers. She loved movies. She loved music. She tried hard to memorize the Qur'an, but thought she started too late. They welcomed our male friends and didn't look at us with suspicion when we walked out of the house with them. My parents hoped their children would closely follow in their footsteps, but trusted us with our own choices.

I'm steadfast in my belief that exploring and wandering are the reasons I know I am Muslim. Learning about Buddhism brought me closer to Islam because it taught me what surrendering means, a lesson none of my Islamic studies teachers have been able to teach me even though that's literally what Islam means. My Islamic studies teachers taught me how to obsess about the mundane—about all the things I'm doing incorrectly which therefore mean my prayers will not be accepted. They taught me guilt. They taught me fear. They taught me that being a good Muslim is difficult.

I never rejected Islam, I just took a break from going through the motions of prayer out of guilt. I wanted to see if I could be compelled to return to my prayer rug. I did. I returned when I felt like my life was empty without worship. I prayed out of gratitude. I prayed and it gave me solace. Ablution became less about splashing water over various parts of my body and felt more like a daily cleanse. A baptism. I stopped obsessing about the small things and my new mantra was "Al-'amal bil niyat," which means, "Actions are dependent on their intentions." My other mantra was "Al deen yusr," which translates to, "Religion is ease."

Exploring and wandering gave me the tools I needed to critically look at the hypocrisy of the 'ulama'a (Islamic elites/scholars/clerics). I realized that I did not have to practice my religion from the point of view of a largely misogynistic group of people. Two years ago, I denounced most hadith (prophetic traditions and sayings), fiqh (Islamic jurisprudence), and tafseer (interpretation) because these three things, all of which play a huge part in how Islam is practiced today, are filtered through the perspective of Muslims born into normalized extreme patriarchy.

I haven't denounced all hadith. I kept the ones that undisputedly made me a better person by teaching me a lesson in morality, kindness, and patience. The two mantras I mentioned above were, in fact, adopted from hadith. The mantra "Religion is ease" is from a hadith related by Abu Hurayra, one of the Prophet's companions, and the mantra "Actions are dependent on their intentions" is from a hadith related by Umar ibn al-Khattab, one of the successors of the Prophet.

I mentioned before that there are many like me. Outliers, outsiders, passing as non-Muslims in the vicinity of other Muslims. When confronted, our stance on religion is waived off as a rebellious phase or an urge to fit in with the dominant non-Muslim society we live in. Despite this feeling of not belonging, we are, generally speaking, not tormented by this existence. We live very healthy, dynamic, and diverse lives. We've established connections and common ground with many different groups of people and we don't feel like pariahs. We've accepted that until a drastic cultural change happens, we're going to continue to lead dual or multiple lives.

I have a new mantra these days, a short surah titled Al-Kafirun (the Disbelievers). For me, the disbelievers, commonly understood to mean those who don't believe in God and the Prophet, also take the form of those who disbelieve that I, too, am a Muslim. The last ayah states, "Lakum deenakum wa liya deen," which means "For you is your religion, and for me is my religion." A simple phrase that holds the power of interconnectedness in spite of our differences. A verse that can empower me to smile at and greet the woman in the headscarf without fear of judgment.

Author's Note: "Practicing Islam in Short Shorts" was penned under a pseudonym, which allowed the author to express herself as honestly and openly as possible. Thanaa was born in the Middle East, but has been living in United States for the last twenty years.

Mahin Ibrahim

How I Used My Hijab to Hide and Why I Don't Anymore

My older sister and I were outside a hidden glass door of a hammam, a Turkish bathhouse. We were there to experience the ritual, born in the seventh century, of washing and purifying one's skin. Up above the glass door was a giant gray, faded dome, made of huge chunks of stone. We had traveled to Istanbul, Turkey, eager to see the world after saving up enough money for a summer trip. I was twenty-five.

"Are we in the right place?" I asked her, as we navigated down a wide staircase with no signs. When we got to what appeared to be the entrance, we found arrows on the floor that indicated women were to turn right. This took us down to a locker room made of stone with black and pink pebbles.

This was no American locker room. Instead of women changing, we walked straight into a group of Turkish women in a circle, dancing, clapping their hands, and shaking everything Allah gave them. One woman yodeled while another clucked her tongue, in what seemed like a festive femininity dance. The women were of all shapes and ages. Some had the build of sumo wrestlers, others resembled tiny fairies.

All were completely naked.

"You didn't tell me we had to be nude?" I yelped. I was terrified of showing anyone my small breasts. The only person who had seen them since puberty was her. I turned back around into darkness. I was getting out of there.

Growing up in a family of six as a Muslim-Bangladeshi American, I was always the flat-chested one. My mother's side of the family is filled with curvaceous cousins much further along in the alphabet than me: Cs, Ds, and beyond. Their breasts and womanly figures propelled them into all sorts of torrid affairs I heard about three continents away. If I was to inherit the family history of diabetes, surely it would come along with a nice pair of double Ds. It had passed down to my older sister, who started wearing a bra at age ten, and was deemed a prized beauty. I, in contrast, was given the part of a small boy in our high school production of "Our Town." I was medically underweight and undersized.

My mother, my Mamuni, took me to a nutritionist to figure out what the problem was. After taking my measurements and writing detailed notes on my eating habits, the nutritionist looked up from her notepad and declared, "She needs more butter." Mamuni dutifully began to put butter in my rice at dinner, which made my previously delicious Bangla meals much less desirable, all in the hopes of fattening me up. It didn't, but it did give me high cholesterol.

After I got my period, Mamuni resigned herself to the fact that I wasn't going to grow. "Well I guess that's it, then," she said, looking at my chest. She didn't bring it up again, but people outside our home did.

In a middle-school typing class, a boy I had a crush on, with green eyes and pale skin, once pounded on the side of his machine and said, "You're as flat as this computer." My crush soon faded.

I would often go to my sister, whom I call Apu in Bangla, for solace and education, lamenting the fact that my chest looked nothing like hers.

"What's cleavage?" I asked Apu. I had a hard time understanding what all the fuss was about. "It means you can push your boobs together, stick a pencil in between, and the pencil won't fall." She demonstrated. I didn't get it. What exactly was so sexy about that? Nevertheless, I tried it. The pencil dropped straight down to the floor. I tried to press my own breasts together. If I mashed them really hard, I had a hint of something.

"I don't even have cleavage."

She tried to cheer me up. "Neither does Keira Knightley. And she's gorgeous!" Apu didn't need to add what we already both knew. I was no Keira Knightley.

+

It wasn't until I started wearing hijab in high school that I found a way to cope. I began to use my religion as an excuse to disconnect from my body. In a time where dating and looks dominate a girl's thoughts, I was different from my non-Muslim girl friends in two huge ways: I did not date or have premarital sex, and I began to wear hijab to cover my hair for modesty and as a declaration of my faith. I had already started wearing long sleeves in middle school, and had covered my legs since fifth grade.

When I began to wear hijab, my understanding was that Allah encouraged men and women to be chaste, but called on women to wear hijab in chapter 33, verse 59, and chapter 24, verse 34 of the Qur'an, where, according to Muhammad Asad's translation, it said, "And tell the believing women, to lower their gaze and be mindful of their chastity, and not to display their charms (in public) beyond what may (decently) be apparent thereof; hence, let them draw their head-coverings over their bosoms." I took this a step further by burying my breasts within my hijab to hide my flatness.

During high school, the more my friends pushed the boundaries of their sexuality and relationship with their bodies, the more I appropriated Islam to hide from my own. *So what if boys don't find me attractive*, I thought. *That's the whole point of my superhero hijab outfit, to repel boys in the first place!* I convinced myself I didn't care about fashion or looking good because I was on a higher spiritual plane, when really it was because I felt like a hopeless cause.

I was so used to pinning the same black hijab tightly around my neck every morning, that I was surprised when a guy once asked, "Why do you wear it like a noose?" I distanced myself from the idea of being attractive or having a body that was perceived that way. I stopped looking in the mirror. Instead, I became a brain with two brown eyes that happened to be attached to a pair of skinny legs. I felt less like a female and more like an amorphous, floating being.

+

Back in the locker room of the hammam, I told my sister, "I don't want to be here."

"We can leave," said Apu.

I thought about it.

If I left, I'd go back to my hotel room, fling myself onto the bed, and make plans to see some other tourist attraction. I'd be safe. I wouldn't have to confront my body and deal with what would surely be awkward eyes fixated on my small chest.

If I stayed, I'd do the exact opposite of what my mind was screaming, and enter into the unknown.

I had come to Turkey to see a part of Islam's rich heritage, explore a foreign country I may never see again, and embark on something new. I was in a beautiful stone and marble building built by the country's greatest architect in the 1500s.

If I fled, I'd leave it all behind. I was tired of running, waiting for the day I'd arrive to a nameless, happier destination I'd chased since I was young.

I decided to stay.

Overhearing us, a woman told me we could keep our undergarments on. That sealed the deal. Apu, of course, fluidly removed all her clothing with full confidence. I deliberated about what to do while the dancing continued; one woman even encouraged me to join in. I said no.

I took a closer look at the dance circle. I had never seen anything like it. The women were completely unabashed with their bodies, it didn't matter if their breasts were too big or too small. They hadn't separated themselves from their bodies as I had. Rather, they were one complete organism, calling on all of their senses to harvest joy.

I took my bra off.

I stored my clothes into a locker and wrapped my body in a peshtemal, a thin cotton towel, I had found in my locker and walked into the bathing room, filled with steam. Directly above was the dome and below it was a huge octagonal marble slab. I hadn't realized from outside, but the dome had hundreds of tiny when I was stained circular glass windows to let light in.

A washer greeted me and led me to a free corner of the heated marble slab, and I sat down next to a bucket of warm water and soap. The washer, a big woman, spoke only Turkish, and so our main communication was when she tried to remove my underwear, which I had still kept on. I firmly shook my head no and kept my fingers tightened on the seam.

Like a Roman tableau, there were women everywhere. I had never seen so many breasts—Turkish, French, American, Spanish, Japanese—all gathered together simply to be washed. None of the breasts, nor the woman attached to them, seemed to care whether I snuck a peek or not, and none looked at my own in disdain.

The washer lathered me with soap and used a kese, a thick Brillo mitt, to scour my skin so harshly I thought I'd bleed. After her initial lathering, she relaxed her hold, and with each exfoliation, I grew more calm, and felt that with every dead skin cell removed, a part of my old, unsure self washed away.

After shampooing my hair, she laid me down on the warm marble to dry. As I looked around, I felt utterly okay that I had revealed my full self. Yes, I have small breasts, but I am a woman, and there is nothing more nurturing than being in a room with women who are all, in a moment, completely content.

It was the first time I made peace with my body.

I stood up, went back into the locker room, put my bra and clothes on, and walked outside. I turned to my sister and looked at her with relief.

Back there with my breasts bare, I let go of all restraint. I decided to be less interested in defining my femininity, or lack thereof, by my flat chest, and more by maintaining a strong, joyous body that can walk, run, think, and love. I focused on being grateful for my healthy breasts that are, so far, cancer-free.

The Qur'an refers to Allah in chapter 32, verses 6 through 7 as "the Almighty, the Dispenser of Grace, who makes most excellent everything that Allah creates." Right there, Allah says it—I am excellent, I am grace, small breasts and all. If Allah had already given me this light, my duty was to brighten it. That meant I couldn't just ignore my body or fight it, but nourish it for its work ahead.

I still wear hijab, but now it's a symbol of my faith and not something for me to hide behind. As my relationship with my body changed, so did my relationship with Islam. I realized I'd been regularly melding my body and mind, without knowing it, through the five daily prayers I've done since I was a child. In one part of the prayer, I stand and place my hands over my chest while reciting verses from the Qur'an. In that moment, my mind and chest are fully connected, and I do this thirty-two times a day. Now I know what that step means. My body had been telling me that it was here to take care of me, and I was finally ready to hear the message.

Though I've traveled further east and west since then, my time in Turkey remains a stark and mysterious crucible. I remember a lot about that trip, praying in the Blue Mosque, journeying across the Galata Bridge, better understanding Turkish women's fight against the government to wear hijab—a fight they won. But my mind always goes back to the hammam, where I first lifted the anchor I placed in the pool of my own contempt, and allowed myself to sail free.

Muhammad Ali Helped Shape My Identity as a Black Muslim

Muhammad Ali was just as Black as he was Muslim, and he belonged to no one. He moved with purpose and helped me unlearn this idea that the Islam I practiced had to be quiet and respectable. Muhammad Ali shaped my consciousness and identity because of the way his faith and activism was just as Black as it was American. He was Black, Muslim, cocky and unapologetic about it.

Any quality I possess is immediately either separated from or attributed to my Blackness. When the qualities are redeeming, I'm separated from my Blackness. When the qualities are considered "bad," they're attributed to my Blackness. When given compliments, people separate me from my Blackness. I'm smart for a Black girl, pretty for a Black girl. I can never be both Black and beautiful. I'm not allowed to be both as a Black woman. I constantly feel like I am being put into a box, I can never be more than one thing at once and I am never allowed to define who I am for myself. I remember being told that I couldn't be pretty, smart, or funny unless someone told me I was.

Muhammad Ali is for me more than just a symbol of strength and radical, unapologetic Blackness. I know how to be confident because of him. You won't tell me who I am, *I* tell you who I am.

Even though it feels like everything has been said about Muhammad Ali, I still don't know what kind of words to use for a man who has influenced my life immensely. Muhammad Ali's life and legacy excite me the same way Beyoncé does when she claims that she woke up flawless. In her saying that she is flawless, she is saying that it's innate. She isn't Beyoncé because she is flawless, she is flawless because she is Beyoncé. (Not that anyone would disagree with Queen Bey.) These declarations of self-love are revolutionary, a form of resistance against white-supremacist beauty standards, and they're radical because they're self-proclaimed. Muhammad Ali did not believe in being humble; he knew he was the greatest, and he didn't try to make people feel comfortable with him. Instead, he told them to get used to him.

Muhammad Ali wasn't a man who wore a thobe and had a long beard. He wore western clothing and didn't speak Arabic, and his Islam was pragmatic. His faith drove his activism and helped me see how Islam can be emancipatory not only for Muslims, but also for non-Muslims. Islam for him wasn't about trying to relive a reality that existed 1,400 years ago; it seamlessly fit the reality he was living in during one of the most violent times for Black people in United States history. His politics, his Blackness, and his religion were all intertwined; they all informed one another.

I relate to his Islam because I don't speak Arabic fluently, I am not Arab, and my Islam is consistently undermined by non-Black Muslims. From asking me how I can possibly read the Qur'an, to whether or not I understand what my name Najma means in Arabic (it means "star"), these deriding comments are menial in comparison with non-Black Muslims using the N-word, or calling Black people like me "abeed."

Anti-Blackness tries to invalidate members of the Nation of Islam; however, it is through the Nation of Islam that Muhammad Ali and Malcolm X found their religion. Islam isn't seen as American and was never seen that way, even though Black Muslim labor built this country. Black Muslims get the short end of the stick when it comes to solidarity in the Muslim world. To exist as Muslim and Black during the sixties in the height of the civil rights movement was radical in itself.

Muhammad Ali not only denounced Christianity but also changed his name from Cassius Clay and claimed his identity as his own. He helped me relate to my religion and my Blackness in a way that no other figure in history could. Nothing ever stopped him from being vocal, even when everything could've been taken away from him. He truly was a champion in and outside the ring.

Something shifted in me when I learned about Muhammad Ali's life, and now I live in the truth of my own greatness.

Of Dark Rooms and Foreign Languages

+

What do you call *fuck* in Arabic? Or *cunt* in Urdu? I have no language I can want in. Is there a word for the georgette of a black abaya against an arm? And does all the Urdu-speaking populace orgasm in gibberish or in complete silence, as they flail to find words in the dark? Or do they just scream?

Urdu doesn't know androgynes and girl-boys. Arabic doesn't know how to blaspheme in grief. To be a Pakistani today is to know half-languages, to always not find the word, to not understand because it had never been spoken. I couldn't come out in Urdu. I couldn't come in Urdu. Being queer and having orgasms, are experiences which I borrow. Without the word, does the thing exist at all?

A professor once said, "no matter how much you love English, you will still dream in Urdu." I would have liked to tell him my dreams have no language. And what does it matter? We'd all like an identity, something to hold onto, something which is nameable and unique. We'd all like to be legitimized. A year back, I wanted to learn French. I really didn't know why, I thought it would be wonderful to know another language. A small department in a popular public university offered classes. Young girls wearing hijabs welcomed us in fluent French. The four-room department didn't exist in real time; it was set apart from the rest of the city. We sat in its biggest room, the library, where the walls were lined with French translations. There were Kafka and Iqbal and Dickens crammed together in one shelf. They came together in a foreign language, in a country of georgette and cotton, outside the brick lane to the department painted with crushed *jamuns.* I don't know how to speak French, as I don't know how to write the Urdu alphabet. But then again, you don't write Urdu, you draw it. I could never learn.

I take this as my coming out. In a language not my own, the language of "the masters," the ones responsible for this ultimate non-place without history or language, a country which is better taken as a phase, something you eventually leave or outgrow. I know no other way. I know no other language. Who do I come out to? The family speaks their Urdu and Punjabi—they have no words for a queer girl-boy, for a lesbian, for a transgender, for a non-binary, for an asexual voyeur—for anything and everything I am and could be. I have no language either for wanting a penis to fuck men with. I lack a language for wanting, for escaping, for whoring, for dying. For fucking, for leaving.

When you were thirteen, you left a period stain on the dining table chair.

Your mother scrubbed it off with a toothbrush as you stood with a bowl of water in your hands. Younger, you stood similarly as your mother ripped off your soiled school uniform trousers with one hand, while trying to keep the bathroom door closed with the other. Women walked past the door, the smell of roses and jasmine wafted over you, and your mother left you inside the bathroom, asking you to clean yourself off. The running tap water made you shiver. You were not ashamed. You ran your fingers down your wet legs, and smiled. Outside, the sound of the نات خوان grew louder.

Now you love to draw patterns in your period blood. Locked inside the bathroom, you squat and bleed on the floor, always a bit surprised with the first drop. You never had a word for periods you liked. Mother called it *menses*, and it made you sick. The Arabic حیض sounded too harsh, like all of Arabic to your ears. But then you didn't have words for most of your body. Much of you has always been unnameable.

Like me, you don't dream in a language. You too have English professors who lament the death of Urdu as if it were something they owned. You speak Urdu with a regional accent, always slurring your ڑ's, and for you English has been a way out. It was a language your parents didn't speak very well; it was a language you could hide in. You would listen to English music, black out explicit CD covers with a marker, and hum under your breath. You could only swear in English, you could only orgasm with a *yes* trapped in the back of your throat. Now seventeen, or twenty-four, or forty-three, you have learned foreign words to name your body. You still don't have a word for periods that you like. Or for the sound of running tap water. Or for shame.

+

I write without hope to a foreign reader. I come out to you, for to you I am legible. But to you I am also unpronounceable. I am nameless in another way. During my visit to England early this year, a woman with whom I made acquaintance would later complain, stumbling over my name for the last time, and ask if she could just call me Mona. I said it didn't matter. Another acquaintance asked me with fascination how many languages I speak. "None, really," I should have said. Maybe a few, but not really. I don't know the words that matter in any language. My country is not really a country. "Country" is what we call it to make it be something. It has no language that belongs to its people, just several languages all half-known and little understood, all borrowed or imposed or learned in secrecy. Would he have understood? I learn new languages to find words I still don't have to name myself, to name who I am becoming, to learn to come out, to make the closet visible or inhabitable, to make it anything, and to move away from the not-knowing, the gibberish, the silence, the mute orgasms. To find words for the want. For the body. For the incommensurable loss.

+

Eventually, you stop reading the smaller Urdu print between the Arabic. You read aloud from the Qur'an because you've learned to find music in your mispronunciations. You no longer try to find what anything means; it doesn't matter. You overlook the Urdu translation. You eventually forget to read Urdu at all. You lose friends. Your professor claims you have a colonial mindset, and that you must decolonize yourself and go back to your roots. You have betrayed something, you don't know what exactly. You try to learn how to say *grapes* in Farsi—*man*, and *thank you*. Immigrant friends teach you how to count in Italian, and you confess you have forgotten how to tell ٢ and ۴ apart in Urdu. You learn French numbers instead. You learn, but you are constantly forgetting. And losing. You no longer remember where your allegiances were supposed to lie. An Indian friend tries to teach you how to say *yes* in Hyderabadi. You have nothing to give back. He will eventually break your heart, and tell you your people are all the same. You have been looking for your people ever since.

+

I could only write this half-naked, my lips numb from hot milk, stopping once in a while to cup my breasts. Muslims love drama. If nothing else, religion does leave you with love for the spectacle. And the erotic. There's nothing more erotic, after all, than the hijab. Young Pakistani Muslim girls famously wear abayas to sneak out of colleges and universities to go out on dates. Girls covered up in black are still seen suspiciously by many; the niqab is worn more for anonymity than for pleasing any god. Some women wear it so they don't have to shave and conform to standards of grooming and hygiene. Burqas are garments for the queer body, for sexual deviants, for young horny college girls. I have worn one many times in the past, especially when I had to immediately go out after a violent bout of ill-timed masturbation. It just hangs in the closet these days. I couldn't give a fuck anymore.

There's no outside of the closet for my people. There are only dark rooms and foreign languages. We don't come out, we shapeshift. Every now and then, you'll see me and I'll see you, and we'll recognize each other from the way our hijabs are pinned tightly around our necks, choking us to some secret pleasure. You'll speak a language I couldn't ever learn, and I'll ask you a different word for چاہت. I've always been visible, you'll tell me. And I've always been so many things I couldn't name. And yet you have known. I have always been legible to you. To the queer girl-boy without a clitoris, fumbling with her burqa, we have always existed in spite of the many languages which claim us. And we have always known our way out.

Neither Slave nor Pharaoh

I wear Abdallah's collar when I'm with Zahid. Abdallah is strictly submissive. Zahid is a switch: he can be either submissive or dominant depending on his mood. He prefers to be dominant, and I prefer that he dominate me.

+

I learned everything I know about being a domme from my experiences with Abdallah. Abdallah is thirty-two, Egyptian, and Muslim. He comes over once a week and stands by my leather couch. He waits for my command. I sit in a big armchair and tell him to take all his clothes off and fold them and put them by the door. Abdallah removes his dress shirt, undershirt, fabric belt, jeans, argyle socks, and boxer briefs, and folds them as instructed. I tell him to sit at my feet, on his knees. He does what I ask. I tell him to lick my boots. He asks if this is hygienic. Abdallah is afraid of germs. This puts him in a bit of a pickle since he's also very much a slave. I tell him to shut the fuck up and lick my boots. He does, and then takes them off and holds my feet in his hands. His hands tremble.

I met Abdallah on Tinder. He was looking for a dominant woman to step on his cock. I was looking for a submissive man who would let me step on his cock. He's here now sitting on the wood floor right across from my chair, on a chain attached to my foot. My foot is on his balls.

Abdallah asks if I want to hear Egyptian music. I say yes.

I tell him that earlier that week, I had bumped into a Palestinian man who said that Egyptians are either slaves or pharaohs. The man was a friend's father-in-law, and he said this not knowing that my mother is Egyptian. He asked me to think of all the Egyptians I knew. "Aren't they either one or the other?" This question made me uncomfortable, especially since it was asking for an absolute judgment about a specific ethnic group. I tend to feel a sense of superiority from people who make generalizations, and this was no different: by saying that people were either in charge or subservient, he wasn't taking into account all the subtleties of power dynamics, of how a submissive person can wield control, of how a pharaoh-like person attains and earns authority.

I wanted to warn him about the dangers and laziness of thinking in binaries.

About how if you think about everyone you know, they can easily fit into either of the two categories of slave and pharaoh if you wanted them to. About how this isn't specific to Egyptians. I wished I could talk openly about how complicated something like BDSM can be, about subs and dommes, but was too afraid of speaking about something as socially taboo as BDSM. Eventually, the man came clean and told me he hates Egyptians because of how they treat Palestinians. He doesn't know how devoted my mother is to my father. That my mother spends her life serving my father.

For years, my father asserted his dominance over my mother, and my mother, a dominant person herself, resisted. But it was in the moments that he was quiet, that he didn't ask for much, that she served him the most—making him tea, washing his clothes, rubbing his scalp, squeezing him fresh lemons over dishes of meals she had cooked, running a lint brush gently over his shoulders before he headed to work. Whenever I spoke poorly of my father, she came to his defense, saying he was a good man. She saw his complexities, and focused on the good in him. She allowed him to financially support her for decades. And if my friend's father-in-law knew that, he would just say it proves that Egyptians are either slaves or pharaohs.

I ask Abdallah what he thinks of this theory. He says he only knows what he likes, and cannot speak for all Egyptian men. I like that about him. Not so eager to generalize. Plus, he wants to be special.

And so Abdallah is sitting on my floor, a collar around his neck, a leash hooked onto his collar. He's got his laptop open, too, and he's working on a lesson plan for his class tomorrow. It occurs to me to ask him if he wants some tea. But I don't want to get up and make it. Besides, he's my sub—he should make my tea. I want to lean in, unhook his collar, and send him into the kitchen to boil water for my tea. If he were white, I'd do it in an instant. But he is Arab, his hair kinky, his skin the color of my mother's skin, my son's skin, and it takes more gumption for me to dominate him—to domme him around. He's told me that his previous dommes were all white. The image of him on a chain at the feet of a white woman infuriates me. Haven't Arab and Muslim men had enough of being chastised, dominated, humiliated, and incarcerated by white supremacy?

I don't ask him this question because it would make me further upset if he told me he didn't mind it. Instead, I tell him he's never allowed to serve anyone else but me, and he lowers his gaze like a good Muslim and says, "Yes, goddess."

I unhook his collar and tell him to go make me some tea. He walks to the kitchen naked and puts the electric kettle on and comes back. A few minutes later, when the teakettle clicks off, I get up to mix the tea, and he asks if he could learn; if I could teach him how to make tea the way I like it. I lead him by the leash to the kitchen, and show him where the spoons are, where the honey is, and how to measure out my black tea leaves. He does, and then we return to the bedroom, to work. A couple of minutes later, I put him on his hands and knees, place my tea cup on the small of his lower back, and pour myself a cup. Abdallah likes it when I treat him like furniture. I love that in my room, with his consent, I can treat a man like furniture.

The next morning, distracted by the thought of him making me tea, by the thought of his naked body, I fill the electric kettle with water, place it on the gas stove, and light the stove. It takes a moment for me to realize what I have done, and I turn off the stove and check the bottom of the kettle for damage. There is none. Afterward, the smoke alarm beeps.

+

Like most people, I had always known about BDSM, but had no idea how it worked. Did domme stand for "dominatrix"? (It doesn't. It just means a dominant woman.) Did dommes have to wear leather or latex from head to toe and carry whips? (They can, but it's not required. A good domme can make her submissive do anything she wants, no matter what she is wearing or wielding.) Did subs, or submissives, love being beaten? (Some do. But not every sub is a pain sub.)

My experiences with pain during sex were all negative before BDSM. The pain was never consensual. Men gagged me, thinking I enjoyed it. They bit my nipples, assuming that because my breasts were large, they were stronger and impervious to pain. They choked me, their hands over my throat, because I asked them to, but none of them had done any training to figure out how to do it correctly, responsibly. Until BDSM, a lot of sex felt like assault. With BDSM, limits are discussed; classes on bondage, rope tying, slapping, choking, and anything else are offered at different "dungeons," clubs, and other spaces. It's almost the sex education everyone should be able to have. I often wish it were.

+

My first shopping trip for kinky gear, I was at a small sex shop, perusing the vanilla section—vibrators, beads, lube. But after walking past all that, I arrived at the leather part, with most objects encased behind glass. Instead of the standard whips and floggers, there were leather and metal cages in phallic shapes. I asked the salesperson if I could see one—I was already seeing it, but I wanted to hold the cage in my hands. She complied, using a key to unlock the case, and placed the cock cage in my palm. It looked like a small chastity cage, and I'd never seen one before. The salesperson told me it was for CBT. I pretended to know what that meant, and then frantically Googled the letters on my phone. CBT. Cock and ball torture. This was a thing.

When I was a little girl, around five or six, one of my favorite things to do was to play a game I called "motorcycle." I would beg my brother, or my cousin, or a neighbor, to lie on his back with his legs stretched straight up. I'd grip his ankles and pretend that the legs were the metal arms of a motorcycle, and then I'd place my foot on his testicles and pretend that they were a gas pedal. I had no idea that I was stepping on testicles, only that they were soft like a small jellyfish and felt funny under my feet.

I told this story to Abdallah when we first met up. His response was, "Lucky boys!" He derives no pleasure at all from his penis being stroked or touched. All he wanted to do, all he wants to do, is please me. His hands quivered when I first allowed him to touch me. I'd never seen or heard a man behave so dutifully, so adoringly. He called me his goddess. I told him to kiss me from head to toe, and he complied, his breath quickening. He loved pleasing me. It's all he wanted to do.

I penetrated his mouth and his ass, because I wanted to, and he wanted to do anything I wanted to do.

I understood right away that being in charge of him was a huge responsibility. I had to make sure that when he was gagging, he wasn't really hurt. I had to make sure his breath wasn't restricted if I smothered him with my breasts. Before we did anything, we had very long discussions over text about what he would and would not consent to. This openness, these clear boundaries, felt nothing like vanilla dating or vanilla sex. It was the vanilla stuff that was scary, I finally understood: often unnegotiated or under-communicated. How many times had I been assaulted in one way or another during vanilla sex? Countless. There was the woman who fisted me against my will; the man who thought my gagging sounds were fun; the guys who thought it was fine to slap my ass without asking permission.

After Abdallah, submissive men began flocking to me. They still do. They tell me exactly what they want me to do for them, and ask me what I like. One sub's hard limit was that he would not do race play. He was white. Another sub's hard limit was that he did not want to ever penetrate me, or have his genitals restrained.

With BDSM, nothing "just happens." Every action, desire, and movement is discussed beforehand. "Please never make me eat my cum," Abdallah had said. "Please never pierce my skin, or make me bleed, or hit my body. Only my face."

Kink meant consent, always. It meant a discussion of boundaries, desires, fears. Unlike vanilla hookups, it meant safety. It meant true submission.

+

Abdallah slowly stopped responding to my texts a few months ago. The silent weeks would be followed by days of ardent messages, begging for my attention. When I gave it, he disappeared again. He was married, it turned out, and I told him that there was no room in our female-dominated relationship for deceit or polytheism. I was a monotheistic-type goddess. When I broke things off with him, I felt a deep sadness. Abdallah was the first good, responsive, and devoted lover I had who, like me, also had a Muslim identity. This shared background made me feel safe, healed me of the years I thought my mother was a pushover, the years of internalized Islamophobia, years that I thought Muslim men were too rigid or stubborn or proud to submit to anyone but God.

I believed I would never find another Muslim person to be kinky with.

+

I met Zahid a year after I met Abdallah, almost to the day. We both serendipitously wore red-and-white striped tops to our first date. I loved this because we looked like a Muslim version of Where's Waldo? Where's Habibi? I had often thought. We talked about everything, including whether kink was in the Qur'an. "When the Qur'an says to beat or whip someone, it never says how hard," he said, joking. "Maybe it's soft play." "Islam means submission," I responded. "I mean, to say, 'I am Muslim,' is to say, 'I submit.'" He smiled and said, "Or, 'I'm a sub.'" We talked about how, in one's devotion to God, one yields completely. To be truly Muslim is to understand that God is the only being anywhere who wields any power. For a believer, her Islam—or her submission—means that she places all her trust in God, and dedicates her life to God's worship. To be Muslim is to be one who submits.

Zahid told me he was hit by a train when he was twenty-three. When I asked him how that happened, he said it was because he and his friends were playing chicken with the train. I wanted to tell him how stupid that is, but instead, I asked him if it was something he did regularly: play chicken with the train. He said yes. He did it all the time. He said that the time he was hit was the only time he paused to think about the train hitting him. He said he blames being hit on that pause. The train hit him, and he spun in place, like a dreidel. He spun and spun before he hit the ground. The spinning absorbed a lot of the contact, so that when he hit the ground, the head injury was not too severe. He was airlifted to a hospital. Four years later, he was diagnosed with testicular cancer. He has one ball. I pull on it gently when he's in my mouth to help him cum.

Zahid's Islam is, like mine, more of an identity than a practice. We spent the first day of Ramadan getting stoned and driving forty-five miles out of town to attend a LARP, or a live-action role-playing game, where nerds gather in large spaces and pretend to be vampires. We arrived too early, and a mile from the exit I began jerking him off in the car. We ended up fucking in a parking lot for half an hour, him calling me his good girl. At the end of Ramadan, he came over, and we drank Eid champagne. We pretended that the label read, "Halal. Enjoy for Eid!" In the morning, I asked him if he thought the pork chorizo I had in the fridge was bad. He smelled it and said he didn't know. I told him I didn't know anything about pork. He said he didn't either, and we laughed. Two Muslims trying to make eggs and chorizo? It didn't happen.

+

In the past year, my gear has piled up. I bought a paddle with a muffled side and a leather side; a long flogger; a crop; bondage tape; an under-bed restraint system. Anal plugs. A ball gag. A harness for my dildos. A black face mask that allows subs to breathe. My favorite thing ever is a dick leash: a leather collar that fastens at the base of a penis and hooks onto a metal chain.

I initially used that on Zahid. At first, I dominated him most sessions. But eventually we switched, and I relished in the switch.

+

The first time I asked Zahid to collar me, I was nervous. I didn't want to be rejected. But I trusted him; we had been playing for five months, and I knew I would be safe if I went into submission with him. He said yes. So I brought out

 Abdallah's collar, which is black leather with red floral stitching, and we stood facing each other. I threw a pillow on my wood floors, the floors Abdallah once licked my feet on, and got on my knees. I asked Zahid if I could look at him, and he said, "Yes." I looked up and he fastened the collar on me, gently, and then hooked the leash onto the metal circle. I breathed deeply. It was a relief to finally be the one taken care of. To not constantly be working to ensure a sub's safety. It was now someone else's turn.

Safia Elhillo

Now More Than Ever

I am telling an interviewer how Muslim I feel inside and he is not hearing me. *But it's more like a cultural thing, right? You're not, like,* religious. *Religious.* The word feels unclean, hurled about to signify a lack of intellect, a disinterest in freedom.

I am full up with believing, I think, but I lack discipline. Maybe nothing about my outside life is Muslim. Nothing Muslim about me that anyone can see. The headscarved girl in college, taking in my bare legs, my bare arms. *You're* Muslim?

The headscarved woman at the bodega, the vastness of her smile. *Habibti. As-salaamu-aleikum. You are like the moon. You are like my daughter. We are sisters. You are like a blossom. God protect you. God preserve you from the Eye.*

+

There is a message from a stranger in my Instagram inbox. *are u muslim?* And an Uber driver encounters my name, greets me with an as-salaamu-aleikum, looks to the backseat to see me uncovered and pierced and his greeting turns to smoke, and for the rest of the trip he will not speak to me.

+

In the days after the election, everyone is So Sorry. Everyone can now point to Sudan on a map. Everyone is well-meaning and Here If You Need Anything and everyone knows to say *muss-lim* instead of muzlim or mozlem or mooselum. Everyone wants to know If I Am Okay. How I Am Feeling. Now More Than Ever everyone wants me to speak into a microphone, type something, give insight to the Real Muslim Experience. I turn off my phone. I sleep, crumpled, for hours, and when I wake it is dusk and the pillow has creased my face.

+

I could tell the story about the white woman by the Columbia Heights Metro station, inviting me to her church, pressing a pamphlet into my hands. *Everyone is welcome,* she promises. I'm a Muslim. *Oh no, honey,* we *believe in God.*

 Everyone wants to hear that it is difficult, that my mother sometimes stuffs her hair into a knit hat instead of wearing her headscarf. Everyone wants to Ask A Muslim. Everyone is So Sorry. Now More Than Ever.

+

I feel most Muslim when I am left alone. My prayer rug is bright red, shot through with gold and turquoise. I see its colors behind my eyes, inside my head, and swell with a magpie's love for its beauty.

+

I fast during Ramadan and by its midpoint I feel charged, sharper. I feel witchy (is this blasphemous?) and clear. I don't know that *pure* is the word, really—just that I feel sinewy, catlike. Everything in my body is a set of eyes. Every feeling is a scream, a revelation.

+

(*Safia* means "pure.")

+

I feel least Muslim when describing, explaining, what makes me feel like a Muslim.

+

I feel most Muslim in the mornings. Or, I feel most Muslim sweating at a party, in the dark, light glistening off the high points of my face.

+

(Everyone wants me to say I feel most Muslim at the airport, randomly selected for additional screening, answering questions about my name at passport control, the gold Qur'an I wear around my neck removed and tucked inside my bag, away from the metal detectors.)

+

I feel most Muslim when my mint plant unfurls new and tiny leaves. I feel most Muslim when my eyeliner is symmetrical. Or, I feel most Muslim when the rice is slightly burnt. When the paving ends and the road turns to red earth. When a body of water perfectly mirrors its sky, a fat cloud looking down at its matching white spot in the river. When I am prey, yes, but mostly I feel most Muslim when my hand is held, when my grandmother takes my feet into her lap, when the breeze brushes past, so gently that my fingertips ache at the promise of touch, or when a plum, cut in half, is glowing pink on the inside, shot through with little veins of gold, and it makes me want to cry.

+

My being hunted did not make me a Muslim. Or more Muslim. The election did not make me a Muslim. Or more. Or less. Not Now More Than Ever. Since the beginning.

Acknowledgments

Rasha Abdulhadi: “Nakba Day Dance” was first published in *Tap Lit* magazine.

Dilruba Ahmed: “Snake Oil, Snake Bite” was first published in *Poetry* magazine. “Ghazal” was first published in *Blackbird* and also appears in *Dhaka Dust* (Graywolf, 2011).

Kaveh Akbar: “A Boy Steps into the Water” first appeared in *Virginia Quarterly Review (VQR)*; “What Use Is Knowing Anything If No One Is Around” was originally published in the *New Yorker.*

Kazim Ali: “Relinquish” first appeared in *Granta.*

Zaina Alsous: “On Longing” was first published in *Glass: A Journal of Poetry.*

Fatimah Asghar: “If They Come for Us” was published in *Poetry* magazine; it and “Haram” appear in *If They Come for Us* (One World/Random House, 2018).

Asnia Asim: “Freedom Bar” was originally published in *Spillway* (June, 2015).

Yasmin Belkhyr: “& My Fathers Relived My Birth,” “Our Mothers Fed Us Well,” and “Sidi Ali” were first published in Bone Light (African Poetry Book Fund and Akashic Books, 2017).

Leila Chatti: “Muslim Girlhood” and “Fasting in Tunis” were first published in *Narrative* magazine; “Confession” was published in *Ploughshares.*

Thanaa El-Naggar: “Practicing Islam in Short Shorts” was previously published in *Gawker.*

Safia Elhillo: “Ars Poetica” first appeared in the *Rumpus*; “Asmarani Is at a Party & Knows This Song” was originally published in *Drunk in a Midnight Choir*; “Ode to Swearing” was first published in FUSION; “Now More Than Ever” appear at Medium.

Tarfia Faizullah: "Self-Portrait as Mango" appears in *Ploughshares*; "100 Bells" originally appeared in *Poetry* magazine; "Aubade with Sage and Lemon" was first published at *BuzzFeed*.

Farnaz Fatemi: "The Woman in the White Chador" was first featured in *Catamaran*.

Saquina Karla C. Guiam: "Tapestry" was first published in *Glass: A Journal of Poetry*.

Lamya H: "Queer Brown Futures (Or Lack Thereof)" was first published at *Autostraddle*.

Zeina Hashem Beck: "Say Love Say God" and "Mother, *Ka'aba*" was first published in Ambit were published in the chapbook *There Was and How Much There Was* (Smith/Doorstop, 2016). "Say Love Say God" was first published in *Ambit*. "Mother *Ka'aba*" was published in *The High Window*.

Mahin Ibrahim: "How I Used My Hijab to Hide and Why I Don't Anymore" first appeared in *Narratively*.

Blair Imani: "Why Activist Blair Imani Will No Longer Wear Hijab Post-Trump" first appeared in *i-D Vice*.

Lily Jamaludin: "For Xulhaz" appeared in the debut issue of *Geometry*.

Randa Jarrar: "Neither Slave nor Pharaoh" was first published by Bitch Media.

Rami Karim: "There needs to be a different word" first appeared in Togvverk on February 20, 2018.

Momina Masood: "Of Dark Rooms and Foreign Languages" was first published in *Minor Literature[s]*.

Momtaza Mehri: "My Imminent Demise Makes the Headlines the Same Day I Notice How Even Your Front Teeth Are" was published in *SAND* journal. "Small Talk" first appeared in *Araweelo Abroad*.

Ladan Osman: "Following the Horn's Call" was published in *The Kitchen-Dweller's Testimony* (University of Nebraska Press, 2015).

beyza ozer: "I've Watched Myself Die Twice This Week" was published in *FAIL BETTER* (Fog Machine, 2017); "Hello, This Letter Was Never Finished," *Powder Keg* magazine.

Khadijah Queen: "Any Other Name" was published in *Poor Claudia* and *I'm So Fine: A List of Famous Men and What I Had On* (YesYes Books, 2017).

Fariha Róisín: "How I Learned to Accept My Queerness as a Muslim Woman" was published in *Teen Vogue.*

Sahar Romani "Burden of Proof" was originally published in *The Offing.* "Conversations with Ammi" was published in Asian American Writers' Workshop's the *Margins*

Charif Shanahan: "Gnawa Boy, Marrakesh, 1968" was previously published in the *New Republic*; "Haratin Girl, Marrakesh, 1968" was first published in *Poetry International.*

Aisha Sharif: "Why I Can Dance Down a Soul-Train Line in Public and Still Be a Muslim" was published in *Rattle.* It, along with "Accent" and "Hot Combs and Hijabs," appears in *To Keep From Undressing* (SparkWheel Press, 2019).

Najma Sharif: "Muhammad Ali Helped Shape My Identity as a Black Muslim" was published in *The Tempest.*

Warsan Shire: "Nail Technician as Palm Reader" was first published in *Her Blue Body* (Flipped Eye Publishing, 2015), and "Midnight in the Foreign Food Aisle" first appeared in *Teaching My Mother How to Give Birth* (Flipped Eye Publishing, 2011),

Saaro Umar: "How to Say" was first published in *Australian Poetry.* "Geography Test" first appeared in *Mana Zine.*

Seema Yasmin: "Polymath" also appears in the chapbook *For Filthy Women Who Worry About Disappointing God* (Diode Poetry, 2017).

Oroolj-e Zafar: "New Names for Brown Baby Girls" first appeared at @*The Fem.*

Index

Biographies

Aria Aber is a writer currently based in Madison, where she serves as the 2018–2019 Ron Wallace Poetry Fellow at the University of Wisconsin-Madison. Her poems are forthcoming or have appeared in *The New Yorker*, *Poetry*, *Kenyon Review*, *The Poetry Review*, and others. Her first book, *Hard Damage*, won the *Prairie Schooner* Poetry Prize; it will be published by the University of Nebraska Press in 2019.

Dina Abdulhadi

Rasha Abdulhadi is a queer Palestinian Southerner who grew up between Damascus, Syria and rural Georgia. They cut their teeth organizing on the southsides of Chicago and Atlanta. Rasha's work has appeared in *Strange Horizons*, *Plume*, *Mslexia*, *Mizna*, *Room*, *|tap|* magazine, and is anthologized in *Stoked Words* (Capturing Fire, 2018) and the Hugo-nominated collection *Luminescent Threads: Connections to Octavia Butler* (Twelfth Planet Press, 2017). Rasha has received fellowships from the Poetry Foundation Emerging Poets Incubator and Maryland State Arts Council and is a member of the Radius of Arab American Writers and Alternate ROOTS. Their first chapbook, *Shell Houses*, is available from The Head & The Hand Press.

Maryam Ahmad studies narrative medicine at Brown University in Providence, Rhode Island. She is a prose editor for *bluestockings* magazine and co-managing editor for *Clerestory Journal of the Arts*. Her favorite pastimes are eating kulfi and getting her eyebrows done.

Beenish Ahmed is a writer and reporter. She's also the founder of *The Alignist*, a venture that delivers multi-sensory literary adventures to doorsteps across the country. She is a former Fulbright Scholar and NPR Kroc Fellow. Her journalistic work has appeared in the *New Yorker*, the *Atlantic*, and on NPR. Beenish currently lives in New York City and is working on a novel about honor killing, YouTube, Islamist militancy, and many different kinds of love.

Dilruba Ahmed's debut book, *Dhaka Dust* (Graywolf Press, 2011), won the Bakeless Prize. Her poems have appeared in *American Poetry Review*, *Blackbird*, *Alaska Quarterly Review*, *New England Review*, and *Poetry*. New work has recently appeared in or is forthcoming in *AGNI*, *Kenyon Review*, *Copper Nickel*, *32 Poems*, and *Ploughshares*. Her poems have also been anthologized in *Literature: The Human Experience* (Bedford/St. Martin's, 2016), *Indivisible: An Anthology of Contemporary South Asian American Poetry* (University of Arkansas, 2010), and elsewhere.

Hieu Minh Nguyen

Kaveh Akbar's poems appear in the *New Yorker*, *Poetry*, *Best American Poetry*, the *New York Times*, and elsewhere. His first book, *Calling a Wolf a Wolf*, was published by Alice James Books. A recipient of a Pushcart Prize and a Ruth Lilly and Dorothy Sargent Rosenberg Poetry Fellowship, Kaveh is the founding editor of *Divedapper*, a home for interviews with major voices in contemporary poetry. Born in Tehran, Iran, he currently teaches at Purdue University and in the low-residency MFA programs at Randolph College and Warren Wilson.

Kazim Ali is the author of sixteen books of poetry, prose, and cross-genre work, most recently *Inquisition* (poems) and *Silver Road* (essays and memoir). He is a professor of literature and writing at the University of California, San Diego.

Nahrain Al-Mousawi is a professor of English literature at the University of Balamand. She has had her poetry published in *Rattle* and *Evergreen Review*, among others. Her articles appear in *Al Jazeera*, *Chicago Tribune*, and the *Globe* and *Mail*.

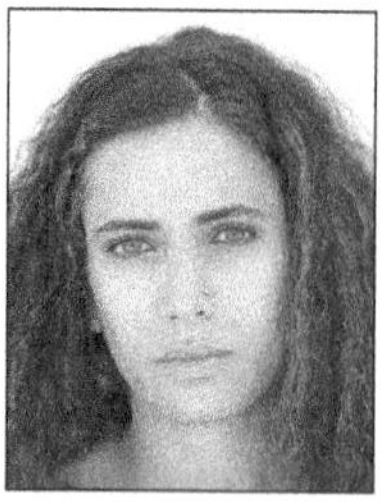

Hala Alyan is a Palestinian American writer and clinical psychologist whose work has appeared in the *New York Times*, *Poetry*, *Guernica*, and elsewhere. Her poetry collections have won the Arab American Book Award and the Crab Orchard Series. Her debut novel, *Salt Houses* (Houghton Mifflin Harcourt, 2017) won the Arab American Book Award and the Dayton Literary Book Prize. Her newest poetry collection, *The Twenty-Ninth Year* (2019) is forthcoming from Houghton Mifflin Harcourt.

Zaina Alsous is a daughter of the Palestinian diaspora. Her chapbook *Lemon Effigies* was published on Anhinga Press. Her first full-length collection *A Theory of Birds* will be published by the University of Arkansas Press in 2019.

Valentina von Klencke

Fatimah Asghar is the co-creator of the Emmy-nominated web series *Brown Girls*. She is the author of *If They Come For Us* (One World/Random House, 2018) and a recipient of a 2017 Ruth Lilly and Dorothy Sargent Rosenberg Poetry Fellowship. In 2017 she was listed on *Forbes'* 30 Under 30 list.

Asnia Asim is the recipient of the University of Chicago's Corbel Scholarship, awarded to graduate students of exceptional academic promise, and Brandeis University's Alan B. Slifka Tuition Award. Her poems have been nominated for the Pushcart Prize and the *Best of the Net Anthology*.

Yasmin Belkhyr is a Moroccan writer and editor. She is the author of *Bone Light* (African Poetry Book Fund and Akashic Books, 2017). Yasmin is the founder and editor in chief of *Winter Tangerine* and Honeysuckle Press. She writes and reports for TED, and is based in New York.

An activist by temperament, the daughter of a Choctaw womxn, **Jacinda Bullie** is a practicing Muslima. Prior to poetics, Jacinda was a natural critic of circumstances, interrogating the world since she can remember. In '96, alongside Jaquanda Villegas and Leida Garcia, Jacinda, cofounded Kuumba Lynx, a Hip Hop Arts collective. Jacinda currently co-curates ½ Pint Poetics, an elementary school poetry gathering, and the Chicago Hip Hop Theater Fest. She is coauthor of a poetic coloring book entitled *FILLINZ. . .Put Some Respect On It!*

Nikia Chaney served as the Inlandia Literary Laureate (2016–2018). She is the author of *us mouth* (University of Hell Press, 2018) and the chapbooks, *Sis Fuss* (Orange Monkey Publishing, 2012) and *ladies, please* (Dancing Girl Press, 2012). She is founding editor of Jamii Publishing, a publishing imprint dedicated to fostering community among poets and writers. She has won grants from the Barbara Deming Fund for Women, Millay Colony for the Arts, Squaw Valley Community of Writers, and Cave Canem.

Leila Chatti is a Tunisian American poet and author of the chapbooks *Ebb* (New-Generation African Poets Series, 2018) and *Tunsiya/Amrikiya*, the 2017 Editors' Selection from Bull City Press (2018). She is the recipient of fellowships and awards from the Fine Arts Work Center in Provincetown, the Tin House Writers' Workshop, Dickinson House, the Barbara Deming Memorial Fund, the Wisconsin Institute for Creative Writing, and Cleveland State University, where she is the inaugural Anisfield-Wolf Fellow. Her poems have appeared in *Ploughshares*, *Tin House*, the *Georgia Review*, *Virginia Quarterly Review*, *New England Review*, *Kenyon Review Online*, *Narrative*, *The Rumpus*, and elsewhere.

Juniper Cruz is a trans Afro-Latinx Muslim poet from Hartford, Connecticut. She is currently an undergraduate student at Kenyon College. Her work has been published in and by *Lambda Literary*, *Puerto Del Sol*, and Poets.org.

Timothy Smith

Safia Elhillo is the author of *The January Children* (University of Nebraska Press, 2017), recipient of the 2016 Sillerman First Book Prize for African Poets and a 2018 Arab American Book Award. Sudanese by way of Washington, DC, and a Cave Canem fellow, she holds an MFA in poetry from the New School. In addition to appearing in several journals and anthologies, her work has been translated into Arabic, Japanese, Estonian, Portuguese, and Greek, and commissioned by Under Armour and the Bavarian State Ballet. Safia is a 2018 Ruth Lilly and Dorothy Sargent Rosenberg Fellow.

Sara Elkamel is a journalist and poet from Cairo, Egypt. She holds an MA in arts and culture journalism from Columbia University's Graduate School of Journalism. Her writing has appeared in the *Guardian*, the *Huffington Post*, *Mada Masr*, *Guernica*, *The Common*, *Winter Tangerine*, and elsewhere.

Rania El Mugammar is a Tkaronto (Toronto) based Sudanese writer, freedom fighter, and anti-oppression consultant. Her work explores themes of liberation, femmeness, Blackness, flight, exile, migration, and home. A short collection of her work can be found in *Our Schools/Ourselves: Constellations of Black Radical Imagining* (Canadian Centre for Policy Alternatives, Canadian Magazine Publishers' Association). You can keep up with her work at www.raniawrites.com.

Thanaa El-Naggar was born in the Middle East and has been living in the United States for over twenty years.

Aaron El Sabrout is an Egyptian trans man who lives on occupied Haudenosaunee territory with his partner and a growing army of spider plants. He is a third-year law student who works on civil rights for incarcerated folks, people of color, as well as trans and two-spirit folks. He is passionate about sustainable food, global indigenous sovereignty, and racial justice. His first self-published chapbook, Migration Routes is available now. He can be reached at @toreachpoise on Twitter and Instagram.

Hazem Fahmy is a Pushcart and Best of the Net nominated poet and critic from Cairo. He is currently pursuing his MA in Middle Eastern Studies from the University of Texas at Austin. His debut chapbook, *Red//Jild//Prayer*, won the 2017 Diode Editions Contest. A Watering Hole fellow, his poetry has appeared, or is forthcoming in *Apogee*, *Mizna*, *The Offing*, and Asian American Writers' Workshop's *The Margins*. His performances have been featured on Button Poetry and Write About Now. He is a reader for the *Shade Journal*, a poetry editor for *Voicemail Poems*, and a contributing writer to *Film Inquiry*.

Sheena Raza Faisal is a writer from Mumbai, India. Her work has appeared in *Vinyl*, *BuzzFeed*, *Jezebel*, and elsewhere. She currently lives in New York.

Tarfia Faizullah is the author of the poetry collections, *Registers of Illuminated Villages* (Graywolf, 2018) and *Seam* (SIU, 2014). Tarfia's writing appears widely, is translated into multiple languages, and has been displayed at the Smithsonian, the Rubin Museum of Art, and elsewhere. Born in Brooklyn, New York to Bangladeshi immigrants and raised in Texas, Tarfia currently teaches in the Writing Program at the School of the Art Institute of Chicago.

Shelby Graham

Farnaz Fatemi is an Iranian American writer living in Santa Cruz, California. Farnaz's poetry and prose appear or are forthcoming in *Grist Journal*, *Catamaran Literary Reader*, *Crab Orchard Review*, *Tahoma Literary Review*, *Tupelo Quarterly*, and several anthologies. She has been awarded residencies from Djerassi, PLAYA, Marble House Project, and I-Park Foundation. Farnaz taught Writing at the University of California, Santa Cruz, from 1997–2018. www.farnazfatemi.com.

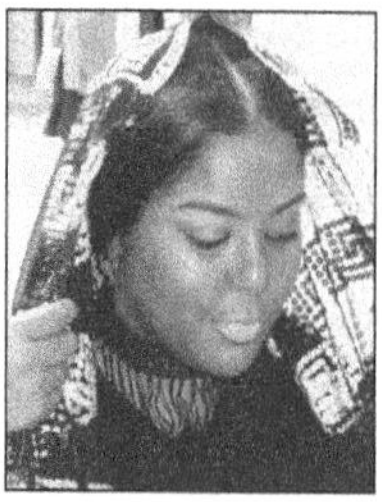

Nina Faith Getachew is an Ethiopian American woman who is the result of everything she's ever loved. She is a practicing Muslim, considers thinking to be an athletic hobby, and aspires to be better than the things she can imagine for herself. She graduated from Temple University. She was born in Rockville, Maryland and is currently a resident of Baltimore, Maryland.

Farah Ghafoor is editor in chief at *Sugar Rascals* and has had poems published in *Ninth Letter*, *Alien Mouth*, and *Big Lucks*, among other places. Her work has been nominated for Best New Poets and Best of the Net, and has been recognized by the Scholastic Art and Writing Awards, Hollins University, the Keats-Shelley Memorial Association, the League of Canadian Poets, and Columbia College Chicago. She believes that she deserves a cat.

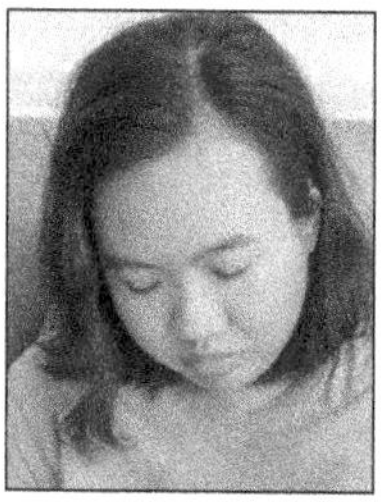

Saquina Karla C. Guiam is a Best of the Net-nominated poet and writer from the Southern Philippines. Her works have appeared in the *Maine Review*, *Outlook Springs*, *Crab Fat Magazine*, *Augur* magazine, and others. She is the *Roots* nonfiction editor for *Rambutan Literary* and an editor for *Umbel & Panicle*.

Lamya H is a queer Muslim writer living in New York City. Her work has appeared in the *Los Angeles Review of Books*, *VICE*, *Salon*, *Vox*, and others. She was a Lambda Literary fellow in 2015 and a Queer Arts Mentorship fellow 2017–2018. Find her on Twitter at @lamyaisangry.

Angelo Aguilor

Zeina Hashem Beck is a Lebanese poet. Her most recent collection, *Louder than Hearts*, won the 2016 May Sarton New Hampshire Poetry Prize. Her work was nominated for the Pushcart Prize, won Best of the Net, and appeared in *Poetry*, *Ploughshares*, *World Literature Today*, the Academy of American Poets' Poem-a-Day, and elsewhere. Her poem "Maqam" won *Poetry* magazine's 2017 Frederick Bock Prize.

Sadia Hassan is a writer and advocate for first generation college students from Atlanta, Georgia. Her work has appeared most recently in *Longreads*, *Araweelo Abroad*, *Documentum*, *The Dartmouth* and *BlackGirl Dangerous*. She is a VONA fellow, a Fine Arts Work Center Summer Workshop fellow, and the inaugural Terry Tempest Williams Fellow for Land and Justice at the Mesa Refuge. Currently, Sadia is working on a book of essays tentatively titled *How to Outrun a Fever* about black girlhood and refugee migration. She graduated from Dartmouth College with a BA in African American Studies and with concentrations in poetry and nonfiction.

Edil Hassan is a Somali-American poet. Her writing has appeared in the *Coalition Zine* and *Asymptote* journal. Additionally, she has work in *A Portrait of Blues: An Anthology on Gender, Bodies, and Identity*. Hassan is interested in how poetry can give word to stories lost by time, generation, and water.

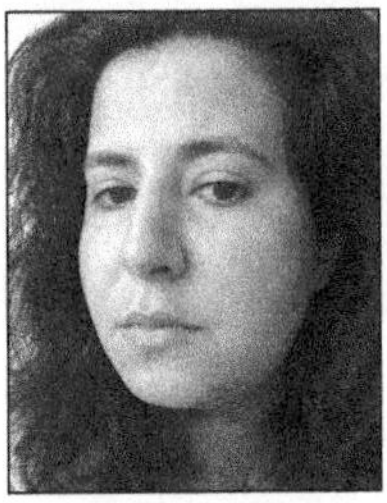

Marwa Helal is the author of the forthcoming *Invasive species* (Nightboat Books, 2019) and winner of *BOMB Magazine*'s 2016 Poetry Prize. She is a fellow of Brooklyn Poets, Cave Canem, and Poets House. She received her MFA in creative writing from The New School.

H.H. is a Black-queer-Muslim-femme poet.

Noor Ibn Najam is a Philly-based poet, teaching artist, herbalist, and freelancer. They are a graduate fellow of the Watering Hole and have attended the Callaloo Creative Writing Workshop and the Pink Door writers' retreat. They are a Pushcart prize nominee with pieces published in *BOAAT*, *The Rumpus*, the *Texas Review*, and elsewhere. Follow them at @sonofstars on Twitter for updates. Noor's poetry will be included in the third volume of *Bettering American Poetry* and *Best New Poets 2018*, and their chapbook, *Praise to Lesser Gods of Love*, was published by Glass poetry press in January 2019.

Mahin Ibrahim is a writer whose work has appeared in *HuffPost*, *Narratively*, and *Amaliah*. Connect with her at @mahinsays on Twitter.

Blair Imani is Black, queer, and Muslim. She is the author of *Modern HERstory: Stories of Women and Nonbinary People Rewriting History* and an Ambassador for Muslims for Progressive Values, one of the oldest progressive Muslim organizations to support the LGBTQ+ community. As a grassroots and online community advocate, Blair has focused heavily on supporting and uplifting LGBTQ+ people of faith, girls and women, the Black community, and the larger LGBTQ community.

Ayman Itani grew up between Beirut, Lebanon, and Dhahran, Saudi Arabia. He discovered his love for poetry in writing classes at Cornell University, under the guidance of his professors Lyrae Van-Clief Stefanon and Valzhyna Mort. After a stint designing educational institutions in upstate New York, he moved back to Lebanon and now divides his time between design and poetry.

Lily Jamaludin is a Malaysian writer and poet who grew up across Malaysia, Australia, Thailand, Romania, and the United States. Her work is published in the *Grinnell Review*, *Geometry Literary*, *plain china*, and *Straits Eclectic*. She graduated from Grinnell College in Iowa, volunteered for Split This Rock, and was a student of the Kuala Lumpur Writer's Workshop. Currently a researcher at a social innovation lab, she also helps run KL's monthly poetry open mic, If Walls Could Talk.

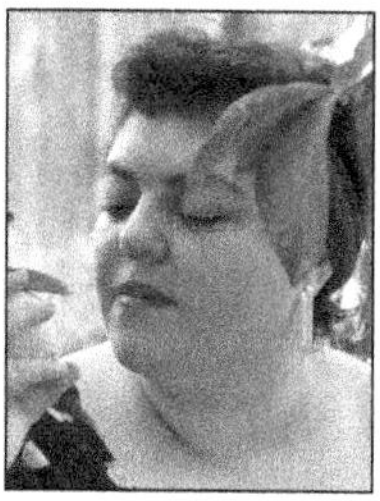

Randa Jarrar is the author of the novel *A Map of Home*, the collection of stories *Him, Me, Muhammad Ali*, and the forthcoming memoir *Love Is An Ex-Country*. She lives in Los Angeles.

Inam Kang is a Pakistani-born poet, student, and curator. His work can be found in *Winter Tangerine*, *Tinderbox Poetry Journal*, Asian American Writers' Workshop's *The Margins*, and other journals and anthologies. He splits his time working and living between Cleveland and southeastern Michigan.

Prashanth Kamalakanthan

Rami Karim is the author of *Smile & Nod* (Wendy's Subway, 2018), *Highway/Freeway* (with Justin Allen), and *Crybaby* (forthcoming, Nightboat Books, 2021). His work has been featured by Press Press, Makhzin, The Poetry Project, MoMA PS1, and Pioneer Works, among others. Rami teaches at the City University of New York and holds an MFA in Writing from Brooklyn College. He lives in Brooklyn and Beirut and is a 2018 artist-in-residence at Cité international des arts in Paris. Other work may be found at ramikarim.com.

Nadra Mabrouk is an MFA candidate in poetry at New York University as a Goldwater Fellow. Her chapbook, *How Things Tasted When We Were Young*, was published in 2016.

Tasneem Maher is an Arab writer who enjoys theatrics in all forms. You can find her work in *Ascend* magazine, *Tenderness Yea*, *Vagabond City Lit*, and more. She tweets sporadically at @mythosgal.

Momina Masood is a writer and film researcher based in Lahore, Pakistan. She edits poetry for *Papercuts*, and is currently researching Pakistni cult and exploitation cinema. Her recent essays on queerness and cinephilia can be found in *Minor Literature[s]* and *DAWN*. She tweets at @momina711.

Momtaza Mehri is a prize-winning poet, essayist, and meme archivist. Her poetry has been featured in *Granta*, *BuzzFeed*, *Vogue*, BBC Radio 4, Poetry Society of America, and Poetry International. Her chapbook, *sugah lump prayer*, was published in 2017. She is the Young People's Laureate for London and a resident columnist at the San Francisco Museum of Modern Art's *Open Space*. Her work has been translated into Arabic and French.

Krista Fogel

Sahar Muradi is a writer, performer, and educator born in Afghanistan and raised in the US. She is coauthor of *A Ritual in X Movements* (Montez Press, 2018), author of the poetry chapbook *[GATES]* (Black Lawrence Press, 2017), and coeditor of *One Story, Thirty Stories: An Anthology of Contemporary Afghan American Literature* (University of Arkansas Press, 2010). Her publications and artwork can be found at saharmuradi.com

Angel Nafis is the author of *BlackGirl Mansion* (Red Beard Press/New School Poetics, 2012). She earned her BA at Hunter College and her MFA in poetry at Warren Wilson College. Her work has appeared in *The BreakBeat Poets* anthology series, *BuzzFeed Reader*, *Poetry*, and elsewhere. Nafis is the recipient of fellowships from Cave Canem, the Millay Colony, the Poetry Foundation, and the National Endowment for the Arts. Founder and curator of the Greenlight Bookstore Poetry Salon, she is also half of the ODES FOR YOU tour with poet, musician, and visual artist Shira Erlichman, and with poet Morgan Parker, she runs The Other Black Girl Collective.

Nasra is a queer, Muslim, Oromo curator/creator living in Amiskwaciwâskahikan (Edmonton) on Treaty 6 territory. They were the Youth Poet Laureate of Edmonton 2016/17 and are currently the Director of Sister to Sister, an artistic showcase for femmes and women of colour and Black Arts Matter—Alberta's interdisciplinary Black arts festival.

Joe Penney

Ladan Osman is the author of *Exiles of Eden* (2019), and *The Kitchen-Dweller's Testimony* (2015). Her writing and photographs appear in a variety of journals. Osman lives in Brooklyn.

beyza ozer is a queer/trans/Muslim writer living in Chicago. beyza's work has appeared in or is forthcoming from *The Offing, Pinwheel, Vinyl, Shabby Doll House*, and the anthology *Subject to Change: Trans Poetry & Conversation* (Sibling Rivalry Press, 2017). beyza is the author of FAIL BETTER (fog machine, 2017) and I DON'T MEAN TO REDSHIFT (Maudlin House, 2016). They are deputy director of social media at YesYes Books. beyza works at the Poetry Foundation.

Michael Teak

Khadijah Queen is the author of five books, most recently *I'm So Fine: A List of Famous Men & What I Had On* (YesYes Books 2017). Her verse play *Non-Sequitur* (Litmus Press) won the Leslie Scalapino Award for Innovative Women's Performance Writing, which included a staged production at Theaterlab NYC in 2015. Individual works appear in *Tin House, American Poetry Review*, and widely elsewhere. She is an Assistant Professor of creative writing at University of Colorado, Boulder.

Fariha Róisín is a writer living on Earth.

Aslan Chalom

Sahar Romani is a poet and educator. Her work appears in *The Offing*, Asian American Writers' Workshop's *The Margins*, and elsewhere. She is the recipient of fellowships from Poets House and New York University, where she received her MFA. Born and raised in Seattle, she lives in New York.

Rumsha Sajid is a Pakistani American writer born in Queens, New York and raised in Michigan. She lives in Oakland, California where works as a housing justice organizer. You can keep up with her at @rumshawrites.

Afshan Shafi lives in Lahore, Pakistan. Her second collection of poems, *Quiet Women*, was published in 2018. She is a poetry editor for the *Aleph Review* and serves as an assistant editor at *Good Times* magazine.

Rachel Eliza Griffiths

Charif Shanahan is the author of *Into Each Room We Enter without Knowing* (Southern Illinois University Press, 2017), winner of the Crab Orchard Series in Poetry First Book Award. His poems have appeared in *New Republic*, *New York Times Magazine*, and PBS NewsHour, and are anthologized in *American Journal: Fifty Poems for Our Time* (Graywolf, 2018) and Furious Flower Poetry Center's forthcoming *Seeding the Future of African American Poetry* (Northwestern University Press, 2019). A Cave Canem graduate fellow, he studied poetry at Princeton University, Dartmouth College, and New York University. He has received awards and fellowships from the Academy of American Poets, the Frost Place, the Fulbright Program/IIE, Millay Colony for the Arts, and the National Endowment for the Arts. A former Wallace Stegner Fellow in Poetry, he is currently a Jones Lecturer in Poetry at Stanford University.

As an African American Muslim woman writer, **Aisha Sharif** explores how racial, gender, and religious identities align, separate, and blend. Her poem, "Why I Can Dance Down a Soul-Train Line in Public and Still Be Muslim," was nominated for a Pushcart Prize in 2015. Aisha's poetry has appeared in *Crab Orchard Review*, *Tidal Basin Review*, *Callaloo*, *CALYX*, *Rattle*, and other literary journals. She is a Cave Canem fellow and earned her MFA at Indiana University, Bloomington. She lives and teaches in Kansas City, Missouri.

Najma Sharif is the founder of the Black Muslim Collective, a writer and visual artist. Her writing has appeared in *Vice, Nylon, Teen Vogue, Bitch Media, Okay Afric*a, and *Vibe.*

Warsan Shire is a Somali British writer and poet. Her debut pamphlet, *Teaching My Mother How to Give Birth* was published in 2011. Shire was awarded the inaugural African Poetry Prize in 2013. In 2014, she was appointed as the first Young Poet Laureate for London and was selected as Poet in Residence for Queensland, Australia. In 2016, she provided the film adaption and poetry for Beyonce's visual album *Lemonad*e.

Saba Taj is an artist from North Carolina or Pakistan. Taj's interdisciplinary work ruminates on mothers, monsters, and *nazar* in the midst of apocalypse. Through mixed-media collage, drawing, poetry, garment-making, and performance, Taj speculates on the boundaries between life-forms and our evolutionary/spiritual potential for porousness and hybridity. www.itssabataj.com. Follow Taj at @itssabataj on Instagram.

Lena Khalaf Tuffaha is a poet, essayist, and translator. Her first book, *Water & Salt,* won the 2018 Washington State Book Award. Her chapbook, *Arab in Newsland,* won the 2016 Two Silvias Prize. She is a recipient of a Hedgebrook Fellowship, and has served as the inaugural poet in residence at Open Books: A Poem Emporium in Seattle. Her chapbook, *Letters from the Interior,* is forthcoming from Diode Editions in 2019.

Saaro Umar is an Oromo artist and poet. Her work has appeared in *Australian Poetry, Overland, Cordite Poetry Review, Expound, Scum,* and elsewhere. She lives in Narrm (Melbourne).

Seema Yasmin is a poet, doctor, and journalist from London. Yasmin is the Director of the Stanford Health Communication Initiative and assistant professor in Stanford University's Department of Medicine. She trained in journalism at the University of Toronto and in medicine at the University of Cambridge. Her poems appear in the *Literary Review, Foundry, Shallow Ends, Breakwater Review* and others. Her chapbook, *For Filthy Women Who Worry About Disappointing God*, won the Diode Editions Chapbook Contest and was published in 2017.

CPSIA information can be obtained
at www.ICGtesting.com
Printed in the USA
BVHW031649270120
570629BV00004B/10

9 781608 466085